EXPLORING SCIENCE

LEVEL 5

ALL AROUND US

EXPLORING SCIENCE 5
ALL AROUND US

REVIEWERS

Dr. Jill Sible: Professor of Biological Sciences, Virginia Tech, Blacksburg, VA

Dr. Giti Khodaparast: Associate Professor of Physics, Virginia Tech, Blacksburg, VA

Katie Rexrode: Science Coach, VISTA (Virginia Initiative for Science Teaching and Achievement) through Virginia Commonwealth University, Richmond, VA, and former 3rd grade teacher, Hanover County Public Schools.

Jimmy Johnson: 5th grade teacher, Elmont Elementary School, Ashland, VA

WRITERS

Jessica Garrett: K-12 Education Outreach Coordinator, Edgerton Center/Massachusetts Institute of Technology, Cambridge, MA, and former 3rd, 5th, and 6th grade teacher

Ben Ligon: 6th grade math and science teacher, Belmont Public Schools, Belmont, MA

with

Joanne Marks: 8th grade science teacher, Belmont Public Schools, Belmont, MA

Jon Marks: 8th grade science teacher, Belmont Public Schools, Belmont, MA

ADDITIONAL CONTRIBUTORS

Dr. Joseph Formaggio: Associate Professor of Physics, Massachusetts Institute of Technology, Cambridge, MA

Dr. Neil Johnson: Instructor, Department of Geosciences, Virginia Tech, Blacksburg, VA

Dr. John Wardle: Professor of Astrophysics, Brandeis University, Waltham, MA

Dr. Don Zeigler: Professor of Geography, Old Dominion University, Virginia Beach, VA

TEACHER MATERIALS DEVELOPMENT TEAM

Lisa Arnold, Richmond, VA • Leslie Swenson, Henrico, VA
Lara Samuels, Richmond, VA • Kelli Domroes, Hanover, VA
Leah Belcher, Henrico, VA

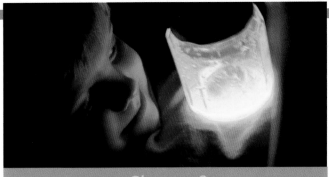

SCIENCE!
SEE IT,
HEAR IT,
FEEL IT.

It is mysterious and beautiful. It can make your hair stand on end, your spine tingle, and your heart pound. Science is everywhere! It is in the ordinary and everyday, and in the rare and unusual. It can happen in a split second or take billions of years to unfold.

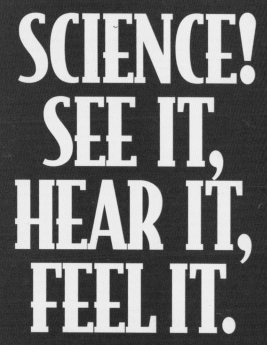

SO MANY MYSTERIES TO SOLVE

- What happens when you blow a horn or sing at the top of your lungs?
How does sound travel?
- What makes a rainbow's different colors?
How do we see light?
- What makes an apple an apple and an orange an orange?
What are we made of?
- How does a rock get stripes of another kind of rock in it?
How do rocks form?

For every question you have, science will try to answer it! We are surrounded by science. It is in the air we breathe, in the blood cells running through our veins, in the crash of a wave on a sandy beach, and in the rumblings deep beneath the ground.

RIDING THE WAVES

This year we will explore all sorts of awesome topics, beginning with two things you might not have ever really thought about—sound and light. We hear and see because of something we *cannot* see—invisible waves. Mysterious? You bet! Fascinating? Absolutely!

A VISIT TO A HIDDEN WORLD

There's a lot more in store for you. You'll explore the tiny, difficult-to-see worlds that make the Earth such an amazing place. You'll learn about the microscopic building blocks of the universe called atoms. When you put them together, they form important chemicals such as water and salt. Put trillions and trillions together and they form everything we can see, smell, and touch—from a kernel of freshly-popped popcorn to a giant octopus.

Another too-small-to-see realm exists within our bodies. You'll explore cells—the unique groupings of miniscule bits that make every living thing special. See the differences between plant cells and animal cells and learn how different kinds of cells are uniquely suited to perform all sorts of special tasks.

Onion cells as seen with a microscope.

UNDER THE SEA AND UP ON THE EARTH

Adventure awaits as you dive deep beneath the oceans' waves to discover what is happening miles below the surface. How did the oceans form? What strange creatures dwell there? What geological formations affect life up here on dry land? Find out!

We will also explore the Earth's surface—the rocks, minerals, and fossils that help to tell the story of our planet's four and a half billion-year-long existence. And what a story it is!

SCIENCE HELPS EXPLAIN LIFE

The sounds of music, a beautiful rainbow, the mysteries of our bodies, the brute force of an earthquake—all very different things. But they have one important characteristic in common. Science helps us understand them. This year is going to be a great adventure, so let's get started!

You don't need a white lab coat and safety glasses to be a scientist. Just learn to look closely and carefully at the world around you.

6

CHAPTER ONE

HOW SCIENCE WORKS

The world is an amazing and complex place, and scientists love to figure out how it all works. They begin by asking a lot of questions. What makes each living thing special? Why do rainbows have so many colors? How can some people sing so beautifully while others make us want to cover our ears?

What questions do <u>you</u> have? It's your turn to be a scientist and search for some of the answers.

7

THE NATURE OF SCIENCE

When you close your eyes and picture a scientist, what do you see? A white lab coat? Bubbling beakers? Think again!

Geologists Andrea Mosie and Harrison Schmitt study moon rocks.

WHAT IS A SCIENTIST?

There is no easy answer to that question. Some scientists work with spiders. Others spend months at the North and South Poles. Some study vast galaxies trillions of miles away, while others explore worlds so tiny they can only be seen with powerful microscopes. There are scientists who design bridges and skyscrapers, and scientists who track the migrations of a single species of whale. Some rarely set foot in a lab, while others spend almost every day in one. When it comes to science, there are no limitations!

WHAT THEY HAVE IN COMMON

Scientists may perform very different tasks and have very different interests—weather, rocks, dolphins, electricity, bacteria—the list is long. But the one thing that unites them as scientists is they have a common goal. They want to explain the natural world. What is the best way to do that?

Good scientists use observation and experimentation. They make models of things and search for evidence to support their ideas. They work step-by-step, using new information and findings to challenge older ideas. They spend a lot of time thinking. They search for clear proof that their ideas are sound, and also look for evidence that might contradict their ideas. Every experiment seeks to gather data to answer a question or test a theory. When you are a scientist, it is okay to make mistakes. Good scientists can learn a lot from their mistakes.

Across the globe, they turn to their fellow scientists both for criticism and for support, sharing discoveries as they make them. They are always eager for new data and new scientific evidence that will help them, and all of us, better understand the complicated world in which we live.

PAST, PRESENT, FUTURE

Science helps us understand the past and shows us how to prepare for the future. It would be awesome if science could answer all the questions we have. It cannot. But what it can do is predict the potential consequences of our actions. If we keep dumping garbage in a river, science can predict how long it will be before all the ecosystems that depend on that river will be endangered. Science warns us that smoking cigarettes will likely cause cancer and that a storm developing in the Atlantic is about to turn into a major hurricane.

Science demands that we learn to respect our planet and all the creatures that share it with us. It also asks that we keep coming up with new questions and continue our search for the answers. Now, it is your turn to be a part of the science fellowship—time to explore the mysteries that surround us and share **your** knowledge with others. After all, **that** is the nature of science!

A REAL MOUSE PAD!
Some scientists spend a lot of time working with mice, using the furry critters to help with their research.

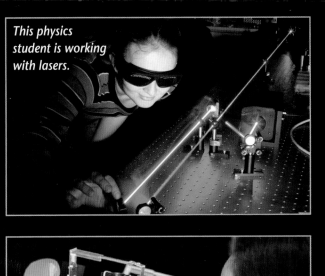

This physics student is working with lasers.

Astronaut José Hernández is also an electrical engineer.

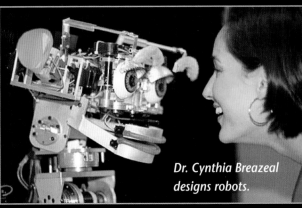

Dr. Cynthia Breazeal designs robots.

Nikisha Patel is a botanist.

Nighttime is the right time for this entomologist. He is studying nocturnal moths.

9

MEASURING MASS
This biologist is using a spring scale to find the mass of a desert turtle.

THE BEST TOOLS

Numbers do not lie. If you are 142 cm tall and see a sign that says, "You must be 165 cm to ride the Danger Mountain roller coaster," you cannot make yourself stretch.

THE LANGUAGE OF SCIENCE

A scientist depends on data. As a result, scientists need different tools to help them measure everything from the speed of light (an amazing 300,000 km per second) to the mass of an adult male African elephant (a hefty 5,000 kg). Scientists might measure the speed of a rocket ship blasting off, the temperature of molten rock spewing from a volcano, the mass of a blue whale, the length of a rare salamander's tail, the volume of vinegar needed to make an exploding model volcano, or the time it takes for a chemical reaction to happen.

Remember the metric system? Numbers are the language that science speaks, and scientists speak "metric." They depend on very precise instruments since many measurements are a matter of life or death. If an engineer knows that a bridge support needs to be heavy enough to hold up a roadway, the measurement of the mass of the concrete pillars had better be accurate. Too light and the bridge could fall down. The wrong data can lead to disaster.

Measuring this?	Use this!
The volume of a vinegar and water solution	Graduated cylinder
The mass of a chunk of granite	Balance or spring scale
The time it takes a NASCAR racer to go one lap	Stopwatch
The boiling point of milk	Thermometer
The length of a page in this book	Centimeter ruler
Your height	Meterstick

MEASURING WIDTH
These scientists are using a centimeter tape measure to find this turtle's size.

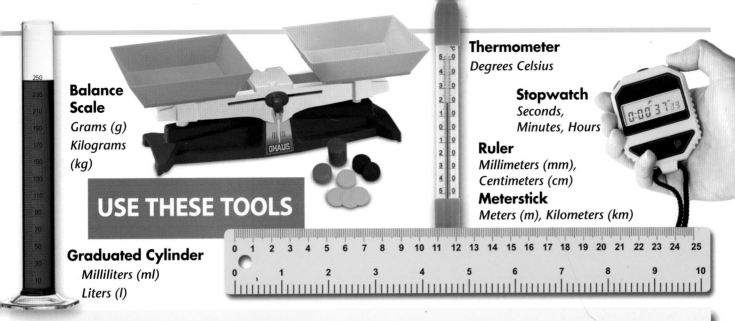

USE THESE TOOLS

Balance Scale
Grams (g)
Kilograms (kg)

Graduated Cylinder
Milliliters (ml)
Liters (l)

Thermometer
Degrees Celsius

Stopwatch
Seconds, Minutes, Hours

Ruler
Millimeters (mm), Centimeters (cm)

Meterstick
Meters (m), Kilometers (km)

ESTIMATING

About as big as a school bus. As light as a slice of bread. Learn how to use the things you are familiar with to help you as you measure.

How do you know what size graduated cylinder to use? Should you use a centimeter ruler or a meterstick? Just how high is 6 meters? How far is 12,000 kilometers? Being able to estimate is a great skill to have. Picture the size, appearance, or feel of these items to use as an estimating guide. You can also measure the distance from your elbow to the end of your middle finger, or your foot from heel to toe, and use those body parts to measure on-the-go.

The average school bus is about 11 meters long.

Estimating Volume

One drop from an eyedropper = 1 ml

A tablespoon of milk = 14.8 ml

A cafeteria milk carton = 240 ml

The biggest size milk jug in a supermarket = 3.8 liters

A community swimming pool = 2.5 million liters

Estimating Length

Length of a pen = 15 cm

Width of a classroom door = 1 m

Length of a soccer field = 90 m

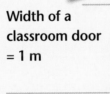

A 10-12 minute walk = 1 km

Estimating Mass

A paper clip = 1 g

One cracker = 28 g

A loaf of bread = 0.5 kg

A compact car = 2,000 kg

Estimating Time

The blink of an eye = 0.25 seconds

"1 Mississippi 2 Mississippi 3 Mississippi 4 Mississippi 5 Mississippi" = 5 seconds

Pictures not shown to scale

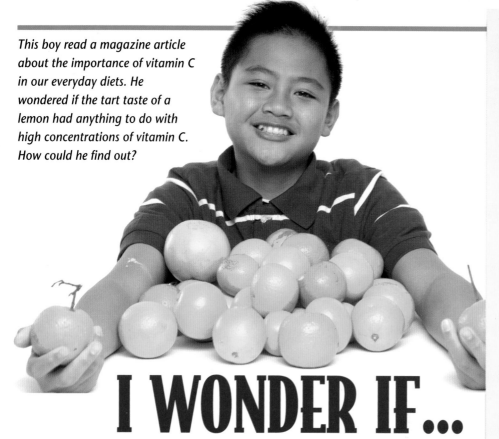

This boy read a magazine article about the importance of vitamin C in our everyday diets. He wondered if the tart taste of a lemon had anything to do with high concentrations of vitamin C. How could he find out?

I WONDER IF...

Reading about science is cool. Doing a hands-on science experiment is even cooler. But how do you start?

Tomorrow at breakfast, look around your house and think of a question that needs an answer. Is your brand of toilet tissue the most biodegradable? Do grapefruits have more vitamin C than oranges? Does one brand of dishwashing liquid really have longer-lasting suds? There are all sorts of possibilities.

Every science experiment begins with a question that can be tested. Some questions are hard to test, such as "Why is the sky blue?" Others might be easier: "Will a toy car go faster with big wheels or small wheels?"

START WITH A HYPOTHESIS

When you have a testable question, you can form a **hypothesis**. Think of your hypothesis as a "cause and effect" statement.

"If _____, then _____."

But here are the tricky parts: Exactly how are you going to test your hypothesis? What supplies will you need? What steps will you have to take? You might have to do some research to find out how to perform your experiment. If you want to test oranges, grapefruits, limes, and lemons for vitamin C, you will need to know how to do it. You have to carefully plan every step you will take.

These students did some research and discovered that a mixture of cornstarch and iodine work as an indicator of vitamin C. When you combine the two, the mixture is deep blue-black, but when it comes in contact with vitamin C, it turns different shades of pale pink to almost clear.

The lightest color will indicate the highest concentration of vitamin C.

4. Design and perform an experiment.

This should attempt to prove whether or not your hypothesis is correct. Even a "wrong" answer can be very valuable.

5. Record and analyze your data.

Write down your results. Draw or take photos of your observations. Repeat your experiments three times.

6. Develop a conclusion and share your findings.

Use charts and graphs to share data. Display your drawings and photos. Write about everything you learned from your data. Cite your sources.

7. Ask new questions.

What have you learned from your experiment? Do you now have new questions? This is where the scientific method starts all over again!

WHAT WILL YOU NEED?

Gather all the measuring tools and equipment you will need before you begin. Don't forget your safety glasses, especially if you are working with liquids. Lemon juice in your eye can really sting! Make sure you have a data notebook handy to keep track of your results.

SAFETY FIRST

This particular experiment involves the use of a stove and a sharp knife so always remember to put safety at the top of your to-do list. Ask a grown-up to help you with your preparations. Safety and science go hand-in-hand.

CASE STUDY: Which type of citrus fruit has the most vitamin C?

Does a lemon have more vitamin C than a grapefruit, an orange, or a lime?

• Prediction

Lemons have the most vitamin C.

• Hypothesis

If an orange, lemon, lime, and grapefruit are tested with a vitamin C indicator, then the lemon will have the most vitamin C.

• Design an experiment

• MATERIALS NEEDED

3 limes, 3 lemons, 3 oranges, 3 grapefruits cut into equal sized wedges.
1/2 teaspoon cornstarch
1 liter distilled water (available in most grocery stores)
tincture of iodine
5 clear plastic cups
Also: a cooking pot, stove, medicine dropper, and graduated cylinder

• Make a Vitamin C Indicator

Pour half a teaspoon of cornstarch into a small cooking pot. Add 0.5 liters of distilled water to the pot and stir until the cornstarch dissolves in the water. Bring to a boil, then let cool. Measure two teaspoons of the cooled solution and 0.5 liters of distilled water into a plastic cup. Using a medicine dropper, add drops of tincture of iodine to the same cup until the mixture turns a deep blue-purple.

Your vitamin C indicator is ready to use. It's time to test the citrus fruits for their vitamin C levels.

• Test the Different Types of Citrus

• *Measure 2 ml of the vitamin C indicator into four separate plastic cups.*
• *Measure 30 ml of juice squeezed from each type of fruit into each cup of solution. The lighter the color after stirring, the higher the amount of vitamin C.*
• *Repeat your test at least three times and record all your data.*
• *Write a conclusion.*

In school, the word "test" might make you a little jumpy,
but in science, every experiment is a series of tests that could help you
find the answers to your questions. Science "tests" are fun!

VARIABLES AND CONSTANTS

Test time! Do those words make you break out in a cold sweat? Luckily, in science you are the one that gets to do the testing. Let's pretend you have noticed that your neighbor is always sprinkling plant food on her tomato plants. Her tomatoes look much bigger than yours, and that has given you an idea for an experiment.

FOLLOW THE SCIENTIFIC METHOD

1. Does the amount of plant food sprinkled on a plant have an effect on how quickly the plant will grow?

2. You do a little research and discover that tomato plants will grow faster if you sprinkle fertilizer on them weekly.

3. Now you are really curious: *If I sprinkle fertilizer on a tomato plant twice a week, then it will grow faster than a tomato plant that is fed once a week*.

4. To do the experiment you will start with six identical small tomato plants. Two will be fed twice a week, two will be fed once a week. Your **control** will be two tomato plants that you will not feed. Soon it will be time to collect your data.

A VARIETY OF VARIABLES

Variables are things that can be changed in an experiment. You are guessing that the amount of tomato food will have an effect on the growth of the plants. The amounts of tomato food are **independent variables**. You are using them to see if either one will have an effect on the plants. This makes the growth of the tomato plant the **dependent variable**. It "depends" on the plant food to bring about some sort of change.

CONSTANTLY THE SAME

Some things must remain exactly the same for an experiment to be a fair test. If you sprinkle differing amounts of plant food on the tomatoes, then perhaps that would have an effect on your results. Some **constants** in this experiment would be the quantity of plant food used, the amount of watering done, and the time that has passed before evaluating any changes.

SPEAK LIKE A SCIENTIST

Variable
(*vair-ee-uh-bull*)
Something that can be changed in an experiment.

Constants
(*con-stints*)
Things that you keep the same on purpose during an experiment.

Independent Variable
Something that is deliberately changed in an experiment to see how it impacts the result.

Dependent Variable
Something that changes in an experiment as a result of a change in the independent variable.

Control
A test where the independent variable is left unchanged to provide a comparison.

CASE STUDY:
Working with Variables

Hypothesis
What are you testing?

A plant food brand suggests adding one teaspoon of plant food to a plant once a week. *If* I add twice as much plant food, *then* the plant will grow twice as fast.

Independent Variable
What are you deliberately changing?

The amount of plant food used on each plant.

Dependent Variables
What changes occured because of what you did?

• The growth of the plant as measured by height

• The growth of the plant as measured by new leaves

• The color and appearance of the plant

Constants
What stayed the same during your experiment?

• Same brand of plant food used on each plant

• Same size and type of plant in each container

• Same type and amount of soil in each container

• Same amount of water and light for each plant

• Growth measured at the same time of day

Some experiments use a control—something that has nothing done to it during the course of an experiment. In this experiment, a plant given no plant food at all would be the control. Comparing the growth rates of the "fed" plants to the control will provide additional information.

ONE IDEA AT A TIME

Remember that you can only test one independent variable with an experiment. Suppose, in the plant food experiment above, you decided to also see if exposure to sunlight made a difference in plant growth at the same time you were testing plant food amounts. You would never know if the plant thrived because of the extra food or the extra sun.

THINKING ABOUT DATA

Gathering data is one of the most important parts of the scientific process. **Quantitative data**—using numbers to express measurements—is really important. But don't forget about **qualitative data**—using descriptions to show how things look, feel, or perhaps even smell. In some experiments, qualitative data can be even more useful than numbers. Make sure to record both types of data. In the plant food experiment above, what was the qualitative data? The quantitative data?

What happened in your experiment? Data holds the answers!

SHARING DATA

You have completed the testing part of your experiment and you have been busy collecting and recording information. Now it's time to **analyze** *(an-uh-lize)* all that data. It's up to you to carefully examine all those numbers and notes and reach a conclusion about what happened. The trouble is, you have pages of numbers and measurements. How can you share your findings with your fellow scientists?

FOR BETTER UNDERSTANDING

The Case Study below shows how one young scientist conducted a tomato plant experiment that tested three different quantities of fertilizer. Would more fertilizer produce a bigger plant with larger tomatoes? Our scientist began with four small tomato plants of similar size. She measured each one, then placed them all in full sun. She also purchased a package of fertilizer especially for vegetables that dissolves in water. The directions said to dilute 7 g of fertilizer in 2 liters of water and feed weekly. Here is what the data revealed.

CASE STUDY:
Gathering Data

Does Feeding a Plant More Plant Food Make it Grow Faster?

HYPOTHESIS: *If I feed a plant with additional fertilizer, then it will grow taller than a plant that is fed less fertilizer.*

PROCEDURE:

Measure and record the starting height for each plant. This will be the baseline.

Feed one plant as directed by the manufacturer with 7 g of plant food mixed in 2 liters of water. Plant will be given 150 ml of the mixture per week.

Feed the second plant with twice as much fertilizer in the water—14 g of plant food mixed with 2 liters of water. Plant will be given 150 ml of the mixture per week.

Feed the third plant with three times as much fertilizer in the water—21 g of plant food mixed with 2 liters of water. Plant will be given 150 ml of the mixture per week.

Do not add fertilizer to the water of the third group. Plant will be given 150 ml of plain water per week. This will be the control.

THE EXPERIMENT: *Plants were fed and growth was measured over a period of five weeks. Watering/feeding and measurements of new growth took place every Saturday at 9 a.m.*

QUANTITATIVE DATA: *A chart was made and plant growth recorded (see the top of the next page for the data).*

QUALITATIVE DATA: *The leaves on the plants that were fed 14 g began developed yellow spots in week four. Leaves on the plants fed 21 g of fertilizer turned brown and brittle and the stem collapsed at week four.*

CONCLUSION: *The manufacturer's recommended amount of fertilizer was the best for plant growth.*

NEW QUESTIONS RAISED: *Will the amount of fertilizer used affect the production and quality of the tomatoes?*

TABLES AND CHARTS

What is a quick way to share all the data you have gathered? Start with a chart or table that organizes numbers in a neat and easy-to-read way.

	7 g	14 g	21 g	No fertilizer
1	2 cm	2.3 cm	3 cm	2 cm
2	3.5 cm	3.8 cm	4.5 cm	2.8 cm
3	4.3 cm	4.4 cm	5.2 cm	3.9 cm
4	5.8 cm	6.1 cm	5.1 cm	4.2 cm
5	7.4 cm	6.6 cm	plant died	5.6 cm

(WEEKS)

New Growth in Centimeters

BAR AND LINE GRAPHS

Graphs provide visual images of what you have discovered. A quick glance at these graphs will reveal which amount of fertilizer led to the fastest growth rate.

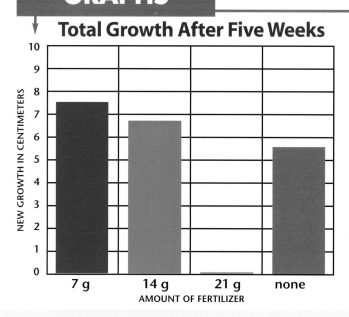

Total Growth After Five Weeks

NEW GROWTH IN CENTIMETERS

AMOUNT OF FERTILIZER: 7 g, 14 g, 21 g, none

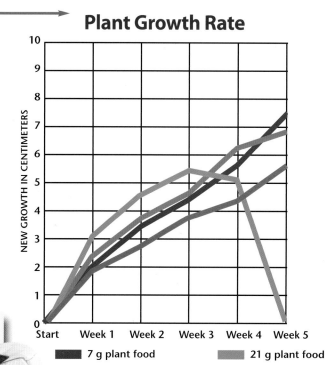

Plant Growth Rate

NEW GROWTH IN CENTIMETERS

Start, Week 1, Week 2, Week 3, Week 4, Week 5

■ 7 g plant food   ■ 21 g plant food
■ 14 g plant food   ■ no plant food

MAKE A MODEL

One way to better understand something is to build a **model** of it. A model is a drawing or a 3-dimensional representation of something. What are models used for? Some help make complex concepts easier to grasp, such as this tooth decay model, which shows the relationship between a tooth, the gums, and bone. Other models solve a need and are used to demonstrate how something might work, such as a model of a new design for an awesome, three-wheel electrified skateboard.

PUTTING YOUR GRAPHS TO WORK

Look at the plant growth graphs above. Can you infer what would have happened if the experiment had continued for another two weeks? Can you see a pattern occuring? One line is headed down and the others are headed up. Read on to find out more.

This student was curious about the structure of a human tooth, so he used a model to explain what happens when a tooth begins to decay.

Scientists have a handy dandy tool to help them understand nature.

TRENDS AND PREDICTIONS

What does this rhino have to do with graphs, experiments, and sharing data? Scientists use patterns and **trends** to help them predict what the future may bring and to warn of danger.

SEEING THE FUTURE

Studying trends helps us see what may happen in years, decades, and even centuries to come. Suppose biologists see that a species is in trouble. How would the extinction of that species upset the balance with the other species that share its community? We can try to rescue a species before it is too late. Being aware of a trend can save lives.

As they test their theories and gather data over time, "pictures" begin to emerge. Scientists in Africa became aware that the population of black rhinos had dropped dramatically each year since 1950. They could predict with some certainty that black rhinos would become extinct by the year 2030 unless they took action. Breeding programs were started and new laws were put into effect to stop the hunting of this fragile species.

SPEAK LIKE A SCIENTIST

Trend
The general direction that data is headed or the way data is changing.

HOW TRENDS HELP IN EVERYDAY LIFE

1. Too Many People?
Population trends are very important to watch. If the birth rate is heading up, it might lead to overcrowding and severe food shortages in coming years. If people are having fewer babies, that affects the population too.

2. Too Cold or Too Hot?
Trends help meteorologists predict the weather, sometimes quite far in advance. Scientists can tell if there are going to be more hurricanes or colder than average winters, for example.

3. Too Few?
Plant and animal populations are affected by humans who hunt or destroy habitats. By being aware of populations that have declining numbers, scientists can work to save them.

CASE STUDY:
Endangered Species

One of the most important ways scientists use trends is in tracking species that are in danger of becoming extinct.

Seeing alarming data can spur people into action. Some animals in great danger now include black rhinos, mountain gorillas, snow leopards, tigers, and leatherback turtles. But there are happy endings for other species, such as the white rhino and the bald eagle, which were saved from extinction by people who became aware of their plight and did something to help. Learn more about endangered species and adopt one!

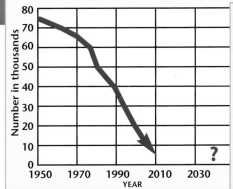

Black Rhino Population

What predictions can you make from these two graphs? What action could you take?

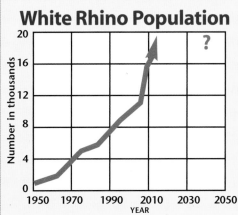

White Rhino Population

NATURE'S FURY

In the summer of 2011, the town of Mineral, Virginia, was the epicenter of a large earthquake. In the months after, there were many small aftershocks. Since Virginia is not in a usual earthquake zone, scientists looked at the pattern of earthquakes that occurred to better understand what may have caused them.

Weather reporters can tell us the forecast for next week, but by studying trends and patterns, they can look much further into the future. They can study data about the ocean's temperatures and predict that it will be an active hurricane season or an especially snowy winter. They can predict at what point too much rain will lead to flooding. Knowing this, they can warn people to leave their homes if they live in areas likely to be flooded. Once more, predictions save lives.

WHAT PATTERN?

Sometimes there are no patterns. Scientists encounter this often. Other times something outside of the expected pattern may occur. A good scientist sees this and tries to understand "why" by asking more questions.

A DISTURBING PREDICTION

There is a lot of talk these days about global warming, and scientists are seeing some alarming trends. Earth's temperature is rising more quickly than it has in the past. Even a few degrees can have a huge impact on our lives. Although some people disagree, most scientists think that humans are causing global warming. Carbon dioxide is a gas that traps heat from the sun, and human activities are creating lots of carbon dioxide. Below are data of how much carbon dioxide is in the air. What predictions might you make about this data?

POLAR WARNING
Melting polar ice caps could affect life around the world, not just at the poles.

CARBON DIOXIDE IN THE AIR *In parts per million*	Year	1960	1970	1980	1990	2000	2010
	Amount of Carbon Dioxide*	317	326	339	354	370	390

PUTTING IT ALL TO WORK

Step by step. No shortcuts. No guesses.
Here's how one student put together an interesting experiment.

Starting an experiment takes thought and careful preparation. You need to do some research and come up with a good question. Then you have to think hard about the best way to answer it. Let's follow one student who began with an important question.

WHAT IS GLOBAL WARMING?

The Greenhouse Effect

Solar Energy

Trapped Heat

Many scientists believe the recent rise in the Earth's temperature is caused by increasing amounts of "greenhouse gases." Most greenhouse gases occur naturally: water vapor, carbon dioxide, methane, nitrous oxide, and ozone. But some are human-made in industry, transportation, and even heating our homes.

One of the prime culprits comes from fossil fuel combustion—the stuff released by the burning of coal, oil, and gas. These gases rise into the atmosphere and form a thick blanket that makes it difficult for heat to escape, so it grows warmer every year. Climate scientists have made these predictions:

1. The Earth will grow warmer. *Temperature changes will affect ecosystems and species must adapt or die.*

Under perfect conditions the sun shines down and much of the heat is radiated back into space. But greenhouse gases trap the sun's heat in the atmosphere where it reflects back down onto Earth's surface.

2. Warmer conditions will affect the water cycle. *More evaporation will increase precipitation in many places, while desert areas will grow even dryer.*

3. The oceans will warm. *Glaciers will begin to melt, which will raise the sea level. Some coastal communities might end up underwater.*

4. Plants will be affected. *We all depend on plants for food. Higher temperatures, shifting climate patterns, and changing water supplies could change the areas where crops grow best. Some crops may do well, but many others could suffer.*

LET THE EXPERIMENT BEGIN

The "nature of science" teaches us that the natural world is understandable. Curious about global warming, this student set out to do an experiment that compared the effect of the sun on water trapped in a bottle and water in an uncapped bottle. She hoped to be able to make some predictions based on the temperature differences between each. How much warmer would water in the capped bottle be? Did being capped make a big difference? She planned to fill four empty 2-liter bottles with the same amount of water and measure the temperature in each bottle. Her hypothesis was this:

If water is trapped in an enclosed space, then it will become warmer than water that is not in an enclosed space.

CHECKLIST:
1. Gather Supplies

All investigations require standard measures and reliable tools. Our young scientist needed:

MATERIALS: 4 empty 2-liter soda bottles, water, 4 total immersion thermometers, measuring cup or graduated cylinder, funnel, safety glasses, pen, data notebook, stopwatch or kitchen timer

2. Note the Procedure

Write down every step of your experiment.

STEPS: 1. Label each bottle: capped or uncapped.

2. Add a thermometer to each bottle.

3. Add identical amounts of water to each bottle. Make sure it is enough to cover the entire thermometer.

4. Place caps on 2 bottles. Leave 2 uncapped.

5. Set the bottles out in direct sun for 4 hours.

Even if you are only dealing with water, safety glasses are always a must-have. Establish good scientific habits!

MEASURE, RECORD, ANALYZE!
Carefully and accurately record your findings. Make sure you take your recordings at regular intervals. This young scientist recorded her data every 1/2 hour.

VARIABLES AND CONSTANTS

Don't forget independent and dependent variables. In this experiment the independent variable was capped or uncapped bottles. What was the dependent variable in her experiment? Does the experiment have any constants?

Our scientist thought about different ways to perform her experiment. How many bottles should she use? There were several different ways to perform the experiment. She chose to use four bottles as a way to have multiple results under identical temperature conditions.

It was now time to start collecting her data.

THE WRAP-UP

As she finished her experiment, she thought about what she had learned. She asked herself: Are there any inferences I can make? What can I conclude? Was my hypothesis correct? What was most surprising about my results?

Science is a building process and good scientists end every experiment with a whole new list of questions.

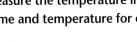

CHECKLIST:
Doing the Experiment
3. Collect the Data

How often will you gather data? What will you be measuring? Science demands evidence!

PROCEDURE: 1. Check the bottles every 30 minutes and measure the temperature in each.

2. Record the time and temperature for each bottle.

3. Note any trends in your data.

4. Share the Results

Science is a complex social endeavor!

CONCLUSIONS: 1. Gather all your data.

2. Turn data into tables, charts, or graphs.

3. Write a summary of what you discovered.

4. Remember to cite any research sources.

CLASSIFICATION

There are millions of different organisms that share Planet Earth. How do scientists tell them apart? They sort them!

Have you ever played Twenty Questions? The first question is usually, "Are you animal, vegetable, or mineral?" Scientists do the same thing, but because they are asking lots of questions, they need a more complex system for sorting. They use a tool called a **classification key**, which is a branching set of choices. All living things are divided into three big groups called **domains**. The next level down is called a **kingdom**. What do you have in common with a giraffe and a worm? You all belong to the kingdom called *Animalia*, which is Latin for animals. Plants are in a different kingdom called *Plantae*. There is also a kingdom just for mushrooms, molds, and mildew called the *Fungi* kingdom and one for *Protista*, which are single-celled organisms.

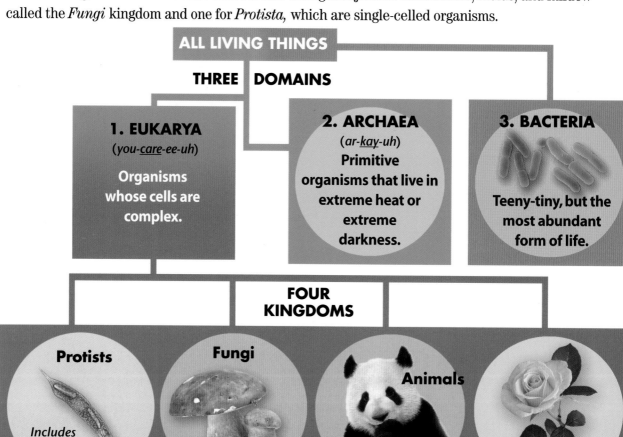

ALL LIVING THINGS

THREE DOMAINS

1. EUKARYA
(*you-care-ee-uh*)
Organisms whose cells are complex.

2. ARCHAEA
(*ar-kay-uh*)
Primitive organisms that live in extreme heat or extreme darkness.

3. BACTERIA
Teeny-tiny, but the most abundant form of life.

FOUR KINGDOMS

Protists
Includes algae

Fungi
Includes yeasts

Animals

Plants

WHAT DO YOU HAVE IN COMMON WITH A GIRAFFE?

Obviously, not too much! But you do have more in common with a giraffe than you do with a mushroom. Each kingdom can be divided into further levels with even more detailed descriptions. This helps provide a pinpoint identification. Each level uses scientific names to identify a particular species.

When scientists talk about a specific organism, they use the two last levels in the sorting process to describe it. These are called the **genus** (*gee-nus*) and **species** (*spee-sees*). Scientists refer to polar bears as *Ursus maritimus*. They call apples *Malus domestica*. A common bacteria that makes milk go sour is *Streptococcus lactis*. And you and all your classmates are *Homo sapiens*. That is our genus and species. It means "wise man" in Latin.

THE "KEY" TO CLASSIFICATION

DICHOTOMOUS KEYS

(Die-cot-uh-muss)

Dichotomous is a big word for a fun and an easy way to sort things. "Di" means two and each branch point has two choices. Here is an example. Take a close look at these insects. Use some of their traits to divide the organisms into categories.

Housefly

Ladybug

Grasshopper

Dragonfly

Let's begin by separating the four insects based on wing type— wings covered by exoskeletons (a hard covering) vs. wings not covered by an exoskeleton (more fragile).

Insects

Hard wings   **Fragile wings**

Round body   **Long body**

Long wings   **Short wings**

Try it with different groups of organisms, such as dogs, sea dwellers, or plants in the park.

These are all types of cats (called the Felidae family) but they are not the same genus and species. Genus and species can make a big difference. You can easily pet only one of these species!

CLASSIFYING ROCKS

Rocks are not living things, so scientists use a different classification key. They place rocks into one of three categories.

1. Igneous *(ig-nee-us)* **Rock**
Molten rock from volcanoes that cooled and hardened.

2. Sedimentary *(sed-ah-men-tah-ree)* **Rock**
Rocks that formed when weathered pieces of other rocks and bits of soil were pressed together and hardened.

3. Metamorphic *(met-ah-mor-fick)* **Rock**
Rocks that have been changed by heat and pressure deep within the Earth.

Which one is the sedimentary rock? Read these descriptions and guess!

RECAP AND REVIEW

THE SCIENTIFIC METHOD

Scientists follow these steps when conducting an investigation.
1. Question 2. Research 3. Hypothesis 4. Experiments and Observations 5. Record Data 6. Conclusion 7. New Question

CONSTANTS AND VARIABLES

All investigations have **constants**, the things that remain the same, and **variables**, the things that can be changed.
There are two types of variables in an investigation.

Independent Variable
The variable that you deliberately change.

Dependent Variable
The variable that changes because of the independent variable.

Virginia's Bald Eagle Population

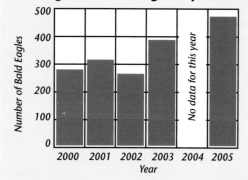

TRENDS AND PREDICTIONS

Looking at data over a period of time may show a **trend**—the way the data is headed or changing. Trends allow scientists to make **predictions** about what is likely to happen in the future. By looking at this data, you can see an upward trend in Virginia's bald eagle population. Scientists can predict that the population will continue to increase.

METRIC MEASUREMENT TOOLS

Length
Millimeters
Centimeters
Meters
Kilometers

Volume
Milliliters
Liters

Mass
Grams
Kilograms

Temperature
Degrees Celsius

Elapsed Time
Seconds
Minutes
Hours

CLASSIFICATION KEY

A tool used to identify objects and organisms.

Use pages 8-9 to answer questions 1 and 2.
1. What is the common goal of scientists?
2. Why do scientists share the results of their studies?

Use pages 10-11 to answer question 3.
3. Copy and complete this chart. First, list the proper tools used to determine the measurements. Second, list the metric unit used to record each measurement.

Measurements	Tool(s) Used	Measurement Increments
Dimensions/Distance		
Mass		
Volume		
Temperature		
Elapsed time		

Use pages 12-13 to answer questions 4 and 5.
4. Explain the difference between a hypothesis and a conclusion.
5. What are the things you need to consider when designing an experiment?

Use pages 14-15 to answer questions 6 and 7.
6. What is a constant in an investigation? What is a variable in an investigation?
7. Explain how the relationship between an independent variable and a dependent variable is like a cause-and-effect statement.

Use pages 16-17 to answer questions 8 and 9.
8. After a scientist collects data, what should he/she do with the information?
9. Describe the difference between a bar graph and a line graph.

Use pages 18-19 to answer question 10.
10. Explain why trends are important for scientists to identify.

Use pages 20-21 to answer question 11.
11. Explain how "nature of science" concepts are seen in the following steps of the experiment shown these pages: hypothesis, procedure, collection of data, and sharing of results.

Use pages 22-23 to answer question 12.
12. What is a classification key?

YOU ARE THE SCIENTIST

A scientist was curious to know if different liquids affected how fast an ice cube melted. She decided to conduct an investigation using water, orange juice, and cola. Write a possible hypothesis for this investigation and then determine the independent variable, dependent variable, and constant(s).

DATA DETETCTIVE

Every ten years the United States Census Bureau conducts a census to determine the population of the country. These statistics are important for many reasons. Create a bar graph showing the data from the chart. Using your bar graph, what can you infer about the homebuilding industry in these counties?

Fastest Growing Localities in Virginia 2000-2010	Population Growth in Percentage (%)
Loudon County	84.1
Prince William County	43.2
King George County	40.4
Stafford County	39.5
James City County	39.3
Manassas Park City	38.7
New Kent County	36.9
Culpepper County	36.3
Spotsylvania County	35.4
Suffolk City	32.8

CHAPTER TWO

WHAT IS SOUND?

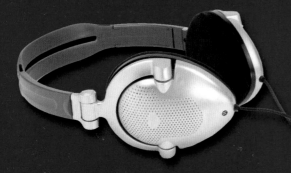

The wail of a siren, a strum on a guitar, a dog barking, the honk of a truck horn—these are sounds we often hear. But <u>how</u> do we hear them? How does the sound of your gym teacher's whistle reach across a big playground? Do animals hear differently than we do?

Just what is sound? Listen up and find out!

A sonic bubble, captured by a special sensor that sees its energy, is frozen at a moment in time as sound energy leaves a violin.

NOW HEAR THIS!

If you get hit by a soccer ball, you feel it, but if a small piece of dust lands on you, you won't feel a thing. Your skin isn't sensitive enough to notice such a small impact. Your ears are amazing organs because they are able to feel impacts even lighter than dust. Your ears can detect pieces of air hitting them. Yes…AIR! Your brain recognizes the vibrations made by air hitting your ears as **sound**. So let's explore what sound is, how it is created, how it travels, and what makes different sounds sound so different.

SOUND FAMILIAR?

Think of a song by your favorite band, the happy noise that a pet makes, or the popping of popcorn. Now imagine the noise of fingernails scratching on a chalkboard or a loud alarm clock waking you up in the morning. Whether you like the sound of it or not, our world is full of noise. In this chapter you will learn that sound is actually a form of energy. You will learn about how sound travels, why your dog can hear sounds that you cannot, and much more.

This sounds alarming!

Scientists aren't the only people who study sound. A musician tuning his violin has trained his ear to notice the tiniest differences in sound. An engineer may use her understanding of sound to invent a better pair of headphones. A doctor might use an ultrasound machine to safely look inside a patient's body. Oceanographers map the bottom of the sea by recording sound waves. Sounds contain information that can warn us, entertain us, and inform us about our world.

It all *sounds* really amazing, doesn't it?

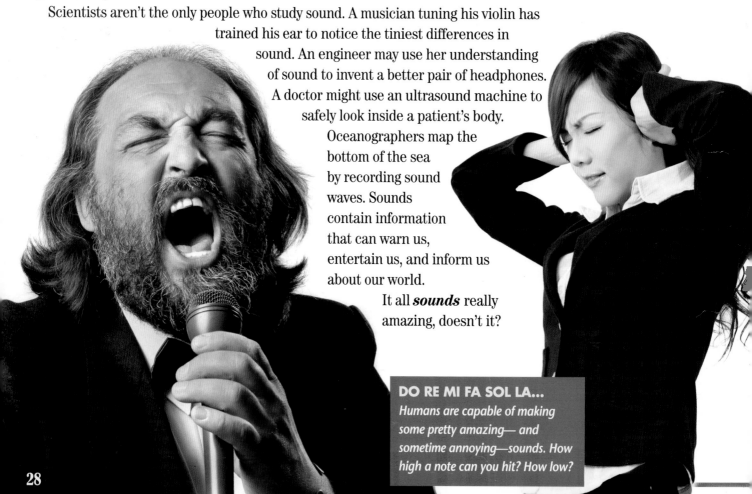

DO RE MI FA SOL LA…
Humans are capable of making some pretty amazing— and sometime annoying—sounds. How high a note can you hit? How low?

KEY WORDS TO KNOW

SOUND

A form of energy made and transmitted by vibrating matter.

VIBRATION

A back and forth movement of an object.

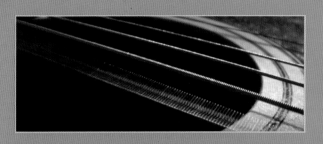

SOUND WAVES

Alternating areas of high and low pressure, called compression waves.

COMPRESSION

(come-presh-un)
The result of molecules being squeezed or pressed together.

WAVELENGTH

The distance between two compressions or between two rarefactions.

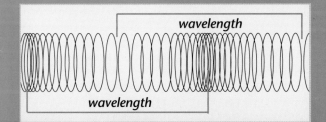

RAREFACTION

(rare-eh-fak-shun)
Places where molecules of air are not squeezed and are spread out.

PITCH

How high or how low a sound is. This is determined by the frequency.

FREQUENCY

The number of wavelengths in a given amount of time.

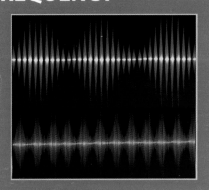

Screeeeeech! Craaaaaash! Hoooooowl! Before you cover your ears, listen to find the answers to this important question…

WHAT IS SOUND?

Most people use their sense of hearing to understand what is happening around them. A person who cannot hear anything experiences a very different world than someone who can. People use sounds in many different languages to communicate ideas, feelings, and thoughts, but sound is more than just spoken words. Music is another sound that humans make. Humans aren't the only animals that make sounds. Almost all animals make sounds, from orangutans and owls to coyotes and crickets. Sounds are also caused by countless nonliving things, such as the crack of thunder, a falling acorn hitting the sidewalk, or raindrops splashing in a puddle.

MAKING SOUND

ROCK ON!
When these drums are hit, they vibrate, which causes the air around them to vibrate, making the thump-thump sounds you hear.

You already know about heat energy, mechanical energy, and electrical energy. Sound is a form of energy that is made and moved by vibrating objects. Sound is formed when a force makes something vibrate. For example, if you pluck a guitar string, the string moves quickly back and forth. The vibrating string bumps into the air near it, causing a wave of energy (called a sound wave) to move through the air. You won't actually hear the guitar make any noise until the sound wave zips through the air into your ears. However, sound travels very fast (over 1,100 km per hour), so it seems like you hear the sound produced the instant you pluck the string.

CASE STUDY: GOOD VIBRATIONS?

If seeing is believing, then try this experiment to see the vibrations that sounds make.

1. *Make a drum by tightly stretching some plastic wrap over a bowl. Use a rubber band to keep the plastic wrap on the bowl.*

2. *Sprinkle some grains of uncooked rice on top of the plastic wrap. Sing, clap your hands, or bang a pot with a spoon. You should see the rice move and vibrate on the plastic wrap.*

3. *All sounds are caused by vibrations. The sounds you made caused the air to vibrate. These vibrations in the air made your drum vibrate, causing the rice that rested on it to vibrate too. You just saw sound!*

THE DECIBEL SCALE

JUST HOW LOUD?

Sounds can range from being as soft as a whisper to as loud as a deafening jet engine. The loudness of sound is measured in **decibels**. It's dangerous to listen to extremely loud sounds because they can permanently damage your hearing. Remember to bring ear plugs to a rock concert!

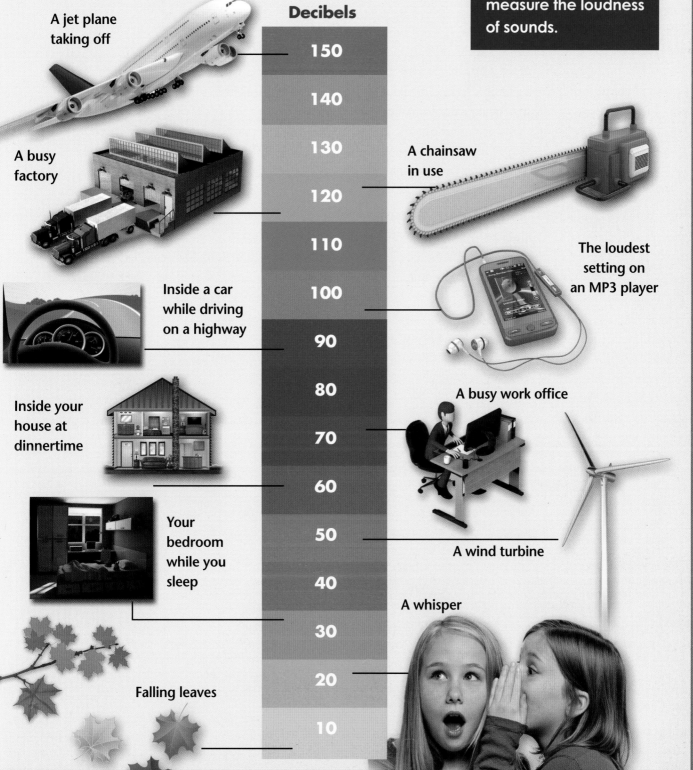

A jet plane taking off

Decibels

150

140

A busy factory

130

A chainsaw in use

120

110

Inside a car while driving on a highway

100

The loudest setting on an MP3 player

90

80

A busy work office

Inside your house at dinnertime

70

60

Your bedroom while you sleep

50

A wind turbine

40

A whisper

30

20

Falling leaves

10

DO THE WAVE

If you drop a pebble in a pond, you will see ripples or waves spread out in all directions from where the pebble hit the water. The energy of the moving pebble has been transferred to the water. Sound waves basically work the same way.

PUSHING AIR

Whenever you yell across the playground or play the piano, you send waves of sound energy through the air. Sound needs something to travel through, so it goes through air, water, and solid materials. Almost all the sounds you hear travel through the air to reach your ears. Air is made of trillions and trillions of tiny molecules of gas. You can't see these molecules because they are too small, but you can feel lots of them if you simply wave your hands around or blow on your fingers. When you clap your hands, you are disturbing some air molecules by pushing them closer together. These air molecules now push against other air molecules, which push against yet more air molecules. It's a bit like a set of dominoes falling against each other.

When the air gets pushed against your ear, you finally detect the sound of your clap. Remember, this all happens almost instantly, so it seems like you hear the sound at the exact moment you clap your hands.

SOUND WAVES MADE SIMPLE

This is a diagram of a sound wave. Notice how parts of the wave are bunched close together. These parts are called **compressions**. *Other parts of the wave are spread out and are called* **rarefactions**. *The distance between two compressions or two rarefactions is called a* **wavelength**.

Direction of wave →

Wavelength

Rarefaction   **Compression**   **Compression**

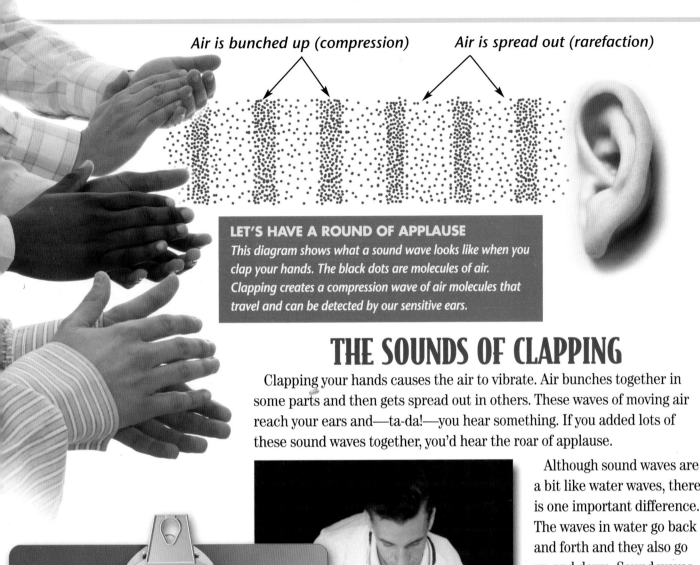

Air is bunched up (compression)

Air is spread out (rarefaction)

LET'S HAVE A ROUND OF APPLAUSE
This diagram shows what a sound wave looks like when you clap your hands. The black dots are molecules of air. Clapping creates a compression wave of air molecules that travel and can be detected by our sensitive ears.

THE SOUNDS OF CLAPPING

Clapping your hands causes the air to vibrate. Air bunches together in some parts and then gets spread out in others. These waves of moving air reach your ears and—ta-da!—you hear something. If you added lots of these sound waves together, you'd hear the roar of applause.

Although sound waves are a bit like water waves, there is one important difference. The waves in water go back and forth and they also go up and down. Sound waves only go back and forth. Scientists call sound waves a type of compression wave, because the air gets bunched up or compressed. Some scientists prefer the term **longitudinal** (*lonj-uh-tood-uh-nul*) wave—but it's just another way to say the same thing.

CASE STUDY:
SLINKYS AND SOUND

Experiment with a Slinky to show how sound waves work. This awesome toy will help you visualize how sound travels.

1. *Lay a Slinky on the floor between you and a friend.*

2. *While your friend holds the other end of the Slinky, quickly push your end of the Slinky toward your friend.*

3. *Can you see the wave of tight coils move down the Slinky? Congratulations. You have just made a compression wave.*

Sound waves work the same way. Compressed air bumps into uncompressed air, moving the sound energy in a forward direction.

SCRUNCHED AND UNSCRUNCHED
This scientist is demonstrating how a compression wave moves. Can you see the area of compression?

Pick up a phone. Call a friend. How does the sound of your "hello" travel from here to there?

HOW SOUND TRAVELS

Have you ever tried to run in the shallow end of a swimming pool? You probably noticed that the water really slowed you down. A weird thing about sound is that it travels *faster* in water than in air! In fact, sound moves more quickly in liquids and solid objects—like wood or rocks—than in air. To understand why, you need to know a little bit about how solids, liquids, and gases, such as air, are different from each other.

SPEEDY SOUND

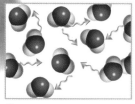
Gas

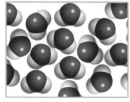
Liquid

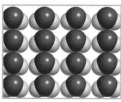
Solid

These diagrams compare how matter is ordered in a gas, liquid, and solid. Notice how the molecules in the solid are packed closely together and that the gas has the most space between its molecules. Imagine you were one of those molecules. Would it be easier to bump into something that is close to you or farther away?

Remember that a sound wave is a compression phenomenon—billions of vibrating particles bumping into each other. One molecule starts to vibrate and bumps into the next one, which bumps into the next and the next. How packed together the molecules are determines how fast the sound waves are able to travel.

When sound travels in a liquid (like water), the sound moves more quickly than in a gas (like air) because the matter is more closely packed together in the liquid. Sound travels even faster through solid objects because the molecules are even closer together. Don't get confused though—the sound does *not* become any louder. It just moves more quickly and can travel farther. Why is this important to know? If you are a whale, your whale songs can travel tremendous distances—across huge expanses of ocean—swiftly. Very useful to tell your whale friends where all the good food is!

SNOOPING SOUNDS

If you've ever tried to listen to something on the other side of a door by putting your ear against the wood, then you've experienced sound waves moving through a solid material.

Humpback whales love to sing. Their songs can travel hundreds of miles through ocean waters.

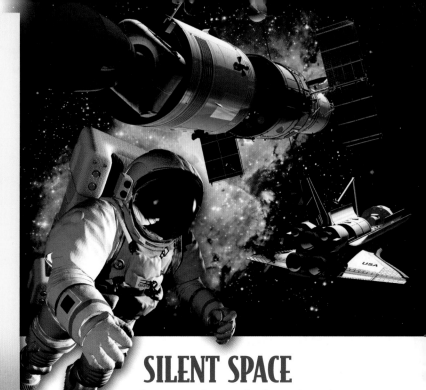

BREAKING THE SOUND BARRIER

When people began flying fast airplanes, aviators wondered if they could go faster than sound traveled, but the blades of their propeller planes chopped up the air and made the planes shake so much it felt like they would break apart in midair. Jet engines did not disturb the air as much, so there was less shaking at high speeds.

How fast do you have to fly to go faster than the speed sound travels—and break the sound barrier? The speed of sound is connected to the temperature of the air it is traveling through, so the answer varies. If it is 0°C, the sound barrier is about 1,190 km per hour. The average jet flies at only about 965 km per hour. Today the armed forces have many planes that can fly at supersonic—faster than sound—speeds.

A SONIC BOOM

As an aircraft breaks the speed of sound, it creates a loud boom because it is traveling faster than the sound waves it is making. This squeezing of the air also makes it look like the plane is passing through a wall.

SILENT SPACE

Sound waves only travel where there is matter through which the vibrations can move. Sound cannot travel in the **vacuum** (*vack-youm*) of outer space. A vacuum is a space with no matter. If an astronaut played the drums on the moon, the drums wouldn't make any noise. This is because there is no air on the moon for the drums to vibrate. Astronauts wearing space suits have to use radios to communicate; otherwise no one would hear them.

Many science fiction movies have exciting scenes with loud explosions from spaceships in outer space. That could never really happen. An exploding spaceship can only make a noise if there is something for the sound to travel through. Because space is so empty of matter, no sound waves can form and, therefore, no sound can be made. That would make for a pretty boring movie, so just remember movies aren't always science.

HOW CELL PHONES SEND SOUNDS

Millions of people depend on their cell phones. But how do cell phones work? Do they send out sound waves? In the olden days, sounds from telephones traveled along wires, and today many home telephones still use wires to carry their messages. Cell phones transmit sound differently. They are actually a kind of radio, and they depend on a type of wave that is very different from a sound wave.

Cell phones depend on a type of radio wave called microwaves, which are different than sound waves. You'll learn more about them in the next chapter. Your friend whispers a secret into her phone. The sound travels through the air into a microphone. Her phone converts it into electrical signals and then into radio waves, sending the message out. Your cell phone detects those waves and converts them into electric signals. The electric signals tell the speakers how to move, converting electricity into vibrations. Those vibrations travel through the air to your ear as sound.

35

From a whisper to a wail, it all has to do with...

FREQUENCY AND PITCH

A heavy truck rumbles down the road and makes a baby cry in the middle of the night. Both the truck and the baby make a sound, but why are their sounds so different? The answer is that they make different kinds of vibrations.

HOW HIGH OR LOW WAS THAT WAVE?

Let's compare the vibrations made by a baby and a truck. Remember, sound vibrations move as waves. One way to describe the shape of a wave is its wavelength. A wavelength is the distance between two adjacent compressions or rarefactions on a sound wave.

Look at the diagram below showing the difference between the baby's sound and the truck's sound. The baby's cry has a short wavelength and the truck's sound has a long wavelength. Because the baby's cry has shorter wavelengths, the cry creates a lot of vibrations in a short period of time. The truck makes fewer vibrations in the same amount of time. Scientists use the word **frequency** when counting wavelengths. A frequency is the number of wavelengths in a given amount of time.

HOW FREQUENT?

Frequency and wavelength are related to each other. High frequency means lots of waves and short wavelengths. Think about how a crying baby sounds. The baby's sound is a high frequency.

← Short wavelength

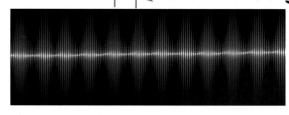

Long wavelength →

Low frequency means fewer waves and longer wavelengths. The truck's sound waves are much farther apart and there are fewer of them, so the truck's sound is a low frequency.

PITCHING IN

Musicians and many other people use the word **pitch** when describing a sound's frequency. The higher the frequency, the higher the pitch. However, pitch and frequency are not exactly the same thing.

Pitch is how a person's ears hear a frequency. Think of it this way: A sound's frequency is a measurable fact, but pitch is more of an opinion. Almost everybody will agree that the pitch of a flute is higher than the pitch of a tuba. When the frequencies are very close but not identical, some people cannot hear any difference. Most would say that the two sounds have the same pitch, but a trained musician might say that the two sounds had different pitches.

THE ENERGY OF SOUND

Some sounds are so loud you have to cover your ears. Others are so soft you have to strain to hear them. Loud sounds, such as a blast on a truck horn or the oom-pah-pah of a tuba, are caused when there is more air in the compression part of the wave and less air in between the compressions. Soft sounds, like a whisper, have less air in the compression parts.

Loud (more air in each compression)

Soft (less air in each compression)

How does a flute's sound compare to a tuba? Think about the wavelength and the amount of air being trapped in each compression.

HOW LOW WILL HE GO?
A tuba makes a very deep, VERY loud noise because there are a lot of air particles in each compression.

CAN YOU MEASURE SOUND?

Just as you can measure distance in centimeters or mass in kilograms, scientists use a unit called a **hertz** *to measure frequency.*

1Hz = 1 vibration per second.

Human ears can detect sounds from as low as 20 hertz to as high as about 20,000 hertz. For example, the lowest key on a piano is about 28 hertz and the highest key is about 4,200 hertz.

The hertz is named after Heinrich Hertz, a German physicist who experimented with light and proved the existence of radio waves. Hertz did not think that radio waves would have much use. He'd be surprised to learn about all the radio stations today! Just remember, radio waves are NOT sound waves.

1857-1894

37

That awesome band you love? Their music is nothing more than billions of different vibrations speeding through the air!

A WORD ABOUT HEARING AIDS

Almost 28 million Americans have some sort of hearing loss that can make their lives very difficult. Some can feel vibrations, but many cannot hear the shriek of a fire engine or a loved one's voice. Medical advances such as hearing aids can help some people hear sounds.

Hearing aids sit in the ear or along the bone behind the ear. They are a bit like in-ear microphones. They convert sound into an electrical current that feeds into an amplifier—something that makes the sounds far louder than the original sound. Hearing aids help many people hear the sounds around them.

GOOD VIBRATIONS

By now you might be wondering why some sounds have a high frequency or pitch and other sounds have a low frequency or pitch. Let's investigate how different pitches can be made by changing the **tension**, length, thickness, and the amount of air involved.

I FEEL TENSE!

Think about a guitar. It has six strings of different thicknesses. The thickest string has the lowest pitch. The thinnest has the highest. The strings attach to a fixed place on the guitar and then each string stretches to a peg that can tighten or relax the tension. Changing the tension on the string changes the pitch too, which makes a guitar play in tune. The combination of tension, thickness, and length make for all sorts of wonderful combinations of beautiful sounds.

CASE STUDY: TENSION

Tension on a vibrating string affects whether its pitch is low or high. Hear for yourself with this investigation.

1. Stretch a rubber band between your index finger and thumb. Don't forget your safety glasses.

2. Pluck the rubber band with your other hand. Experiment with the different pitches you can make by pulling the rubber band more tightly or having it be more loose.

3. Put a chair leg inside the rubber band, and then really stretch the rubber band out. Try plucking it now. How many different pitches can you hear?

WHAT HAPPENS? When the tension increases, does the pitch get higher or lower? What happens to the pitch If the tension decreases?

CASE STUDY: AIR AND PITCH

The amount of air that vibrates affects whether a pitch is high or low. Prove it with this investigation.

1. Get several identical plastic bottles.

2. Fill each with a different amount of water.

3. Arrange the bottles in order from least full to most full.

4. Blow across the top of one of the bottles to hear a pitch. You may have to experiment with the best position to make a sound.

5. Blow across each bottle to listen to the different pitches that can be made. If you adjust the water levels, you can actually create a musical scale!

WHAT HAPPENS?
Does a short column of air produce a higher pitch than a long column of air?

CASE STUDY: LENGTH

The length of a vibrating object affects whether its pitch is low or high. Get several identical nails and your safety glasses. Then try this, and listen!

1. With a grown-up's help, carefully use a hammer to nail several nails into a block of wood so the nails are different heights. Keep the nails a few cm apart. It will probably be easier if you hammer the first nail in the deepest, and every other nail a little less deep.

2. Once all nails are secure, hit each nail, one by one, with a pencil and listen to the different sounds.

WHAT HAPPENS? When the length of an object increases, does the pitch get lower or higher? If the length decreases, what happens to the pitch?

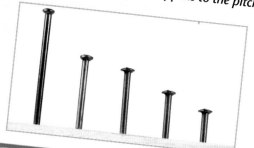

CASE STUDY: THICKNESS

The thickness of a vibrating object affects whether its pitch is low or high. Prove it!

1. With a grown-up's help, carefully use a hammer to nail several nails of different thicknesses into a block of wood. Keep the nails at the same height. The nails should be a few cm apart.

2. Once all nails are secure, hit each nail, one by one, with a pencil and listen to the different sounds.

WHAT HAPPENS? When the thickness of an object increases, does the pitch get lower or higher? If the thickness decreases, what happens to the pitch?

Are these giraffes "talking" behind your back?

MAKING SOUNDS

For a long time, scientists thought that giraffes were mute and made no sounds at all. Animal experts were puzzled. How were these super-tall, silent giraffes communicating with each other?

WHAT'S YOUR FREQUENCY?

The mystery was solved when scientists discovered that giraffes make sounds that are so low that humans cannot hear them. Remember that the frequency of a sound wave is the number of wavelengths in a given amount of time and is measured in hertz. Human ears can hear frequencies between 20 hertz and 20,000 hertz. Scientists discovered that giraffes produce frequencies that are less than 20 hertz. When giraffes want to warn each other about predators or are trying to locate their babies, they make sounds that we simply cannot hear.

It turns out giraffes are not alone as "low-talkers." They have lots of company.

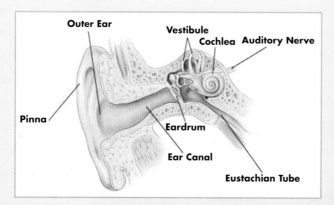

Vocal Chords

Larynx

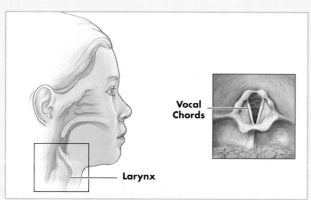

Outer Ear

Vestibule

Cochlea   Auditory Nerve

Pinna

Eardrum

Ear Canal

Eustachian Tube

HOW YOUR BODY MAKES SOUNDS

If you want to speak, cry, laugh, or sing, you must use your larynx (lair-inks). Your larynx is located at the top of your windpipe and contains your vocal cords. When you want to make a sound, stretchy bands in your vocal chords vibrate and send sound waves through the air.

HOW YOUR BODY HEARS SOUNDS

Your eardrum is a thin layer inside your ear. When air particles vibrate against your eardrum, they are vibrating against the smallest bones in your body—your three tiny ear bones. How small are they? The smallest bone is only about 0.25 cm long. Vibrations from your ear bones are sent through nerves to your brain, which converts the signal into a sound.

HOW LOW CAN YOU GO?

Any sound that is below 20 hertz is called **infrasound**. Giraffes are not the only animals that can detect infrasound. Elephants, alligators, hippos, and rhinoceroses are other animals that communicate with infrasound. For example, elephants can hear down to 16 hertz. An advantage of infrasound is that it can travel really far, so these animals are able to talk to each other over large distances. The next time you visit the zoo, ask yourself if that elephant is yawning or is it saying something that's just too low a frequency for you to hear.

"Elephantese" includes sounds that humans cannot hear.

HOW HIGH CAN YOU HEAR?

If you've spent a lot of time around dogs, you might have seen a dog whistle, but you would not have heard it. That's because a dog whistle creates a pitch that is so high, humans cannot hear it. Dogs can hear between 40 and 60,000 hertz. This means that dogs can't hear the very lowest keys on a piano, but they can hear sounds that are about three times as high as we can hear. A sound that is above 20,000 hertz is called **ultrasound**. Dog whistles allow humans to send signals to dogs that other humans cannot hear. Many animals are able to hear frequencies much higher than humans. Cats can hear ultrasounds as high as 60,000 hertz. Bats can hear up to 150,000 hertz. And dolphins can hear higher than 150,000 hertz. There's a lot of chatter going on out there that our ears are unable to hear.

A big-eared bat

Hertz in thousands

	0	20	40	60	80	100	120	140	160	180
Humans										
Dogs										
Cats										
Bats										
Dolphins										
Whales										
Elephants										

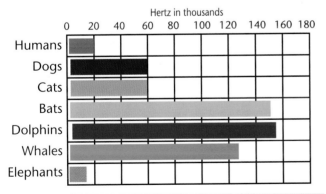

HUMANS USE ULTRASOUND TOO
Doctors depend on ultrasound machines that use high frequency sound waves and their echoes—just like the echolocation used by bats, whales, and dolphins—to peer deep inside the human body.

IS THERE AN ECHO IN HERE?

Have you ever played the game "Marco Polo" in a swimming pool? If you are "it," you close your eyes and yell out, "Marco." Your friends shout back, "Polo," which gives you clues to where they are hiding. You have to use sound to make a mental map. Bats, dolphins, and toothed whales use sound in a similar way. Bats hunt at night and dolphins and toothed whales often hunt in dark, murky waters. All three use **echolocation** *(eck-oh-low-<u>kay</u>-shun) to find prey and navigate.*

Here's how it works. Animals that depend on echolocation make high-pitched, ultrasonic squeaks. These sound waves go out in all directions and reflect or echo back to the bat, dolphin, or toothed whale that has made them. The animals then use these echoes to hear (not see) what's around them—including their prey.

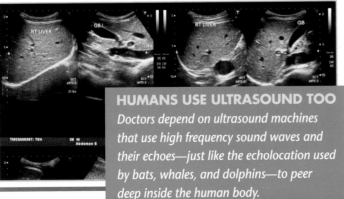

Has anyone ever told you to stop making so much noise?
What makes some sounds so awful and other sounds so beautiful?

MAKING MUSIC

Most people don't listen to recordings of the slam of car doors shutting, the thud of backpacks hitting the ground, or the churn of washing machines. When sounds create irregular mixtures of vibrations, they do not sound pleasant together. Most people prefer the sounds of flutes, guitars, and saxophones. Why? The answer lies in the waves. Noise is random sounds that are unpleasant to listen to, while music is sound that follows a pattern.

Not everyone likes the same pattern of music, but we can all tell the difference between noise and a beautiful piano sonata because of the wave patterns. Let's explore the ways that different types of instruments make sounds.

ARE YOU IN TUNE?
If you strike a tuning fork, it will vibrate and produce a musical note. This fork makes 440 hertz—the musical note "A."

IS IT NOISE OR MUSIC?

Think of a pleasant sound, perhaps a bird tweeting or a flute playing. Those sounds have a regular wave pattern. The pattern repeats over and over.

In an unpleasant sound—such as jackhammer—the waves of noise are irregular. They do not have a repeated pattern.

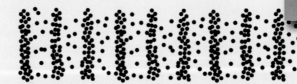

Can you see how disorganized the noisy waves are? No wonder they are so unpleasant to listen to!

42

PERCUSSION

The percussion family includes a wide range of different looking instruments including the drums, triangle, xylophone, and cymbals. Musicians make sounds with percussion instruments by striking or shaking the instrument. When hit, the instrument itself vibrates, creating sound waves. Some percussion instruments create a definite pitch, while others, such as snare drums and maracas, produce so many frequencies that they have no real pitch.

WOODWINDS

What do a flute, saxophone, oboe, piccolo, and clarinet have in common? They are all members of the woodwind family. This means that they are basically pipes that are blown into or across. The pipe part of the instrument contains a long, thin column of air. When the musician blows on a woodwind, the air inside the pipe vibrates. These instruments have holes in them that the musician can open or close with fingers to change the length of the pipe. The longer the column of air, the deeper the pitch. If the pipe is shortened, the pitch gets higher. Some woodwinds, like the clarinet, use a reed—a thin piece of wood—which the musician blows on to vibrate the air.

Which will produce a higher sound?

BRASS

These shiny instruments include trumpets, trombones, French horns, and tubas. The secret to playing these is all in the lips. Musicians put their mouths against the mouthpiece and blow in such a way that their lips vibrate. Brass instruments can produce different pitches by changing the length of tubing the air moves through. Trumpets have valves that serve this purpose; a trombone is stretched apart or pulled inward to create different pitches.

STRINGS

Instruments like guitars, pianos, and violins create sounds when a string is plucked (guitar), struck (piano), or has a bow drawn against it (violin). These instruments have a variety of strings, each having a different thickness. Thinner strings produce higher pitches than thicker strings. Musicians use their fingers to shorten the strings of violins and guitars to produce higher pitches.

RECAP AND REVIEW

SOUND

Sound is what we hear when matter vibrates. Sound is energy.
Sound travels in **compression waves**.

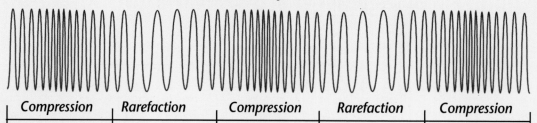

| Compression | Rarefaction | Compression | Rarefaction | Compression |

WAVELENGTH

The distance between two compressions or two rarefactions

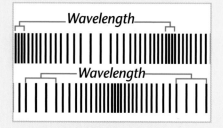

FREQUENCY

The number of wavelengths in a given unit of time

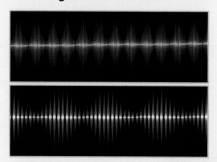

PITCH

How high or low a sound is

REMEMBER!

High Frequency = High Pitch
Low Frequency = Low Pitch

Sound waves only travel where there is matter to transmit them. They need something to carry the vibration.

GASES
Sound travels slowly because the molecules are farther apart.

LIQUIDS
Sound travels faster because the molecules are closer together.

SOLIDS
Sound travels fastest because the molecules are very close together.

MUSICAL INSTRUMENTS VIBRATE TO PRODUCE SOUND

Woodwind = Vibrating air
Percussion = Vibrating surfaces
Brass = Vibrating lips
Strings = Vibrating strings

WHAT CAN WE HEAR?

Humans: 20-20,000 Hz
Bats: 20-150,000 Hz
Dogs: 40-60,000 Hz
Beluga whale: 1,000-123,000 Hz

Use pages 28-29 to answer questions 1-3.

1. How do ears detect sound?

2. How do people in different professions use sounds?

3. What is sound?

Use pages 30-31 to answer questions 4 and 5.

4. Use the words **vibrate** and **force** to describe how sound is made.

5. What do decibels measure?

Use pages 32-33 to answer questions 6 and 7.

6. Why is a sound wave called a compression (longitudinal) wave?

7. Study the sound wave seen here. What does the letter A show? What does the letter B show?

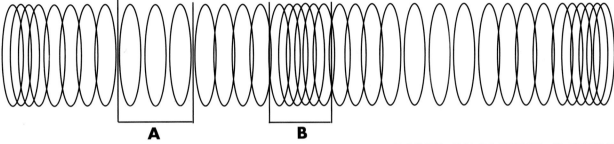

A   **B**

Use pages 34-35 to answer questions 8 and 9.

8. Describe how sound travels in a gas, liquid, and solid. In which state of matter does sound travel fastest?

9. Why can't sound travel in space?

Use pages 36-37 to answer question 10.

10. Explain the relationship between frequency and pitch.

Use pages 38-39 to answer question 11.

11. Sketch four images to illustrate how each of the following affects the pitch of a vibrating object: tension, thickness, air and pitch, and length. You may also choose to describe these using complete sentences.

Use pages 40-41 to answer question 12.

12. Compare and contrast the sounds humans create and hear to those of other animals.

Use pages 42-43 to answer question 13.

13. Create a chart to explain and describe how each group of musical instruments produces sound.

YOU ARE THE SCIENTIST

If Earth was in need of a non-electric communication system, how might people be able to communicate over long distances without physically traveling from one place to another? Think like a scientist and use what you know about how sound travels through different states of matter to design this new communication system. Why would this idea be effective?

DATA DETETCTIVE

Four million workers go to work each day in places where the noise level is so high it can damage hearing. Carpenters face an especially high risk. Based on this graph, which power tool is the most dangerous for hearing-health.

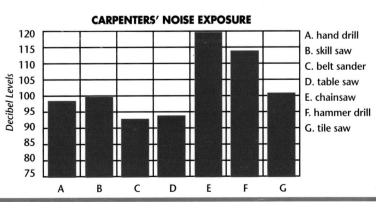

CARPENTERS' NOISE EXPOSURE

A. hand drill
B. skill saw
C. belt sander
D. table saw
E. chainsaw
F. hammer drill
G. tile saw

CHAPTER THREE

WHAT IS LIGHT?

This beautiful rainbow is made of light and water and nothing more. Huge rainbows that arc across the entire sky are rare because they can only form when the sun is out during a rain shower. As the sunlight shines on the raindrops, the many colors within sunlight are revealed. How does it happen? Read on!

Have you ever looked at a rainbow and wondered how it was created? Where did all those brilliant colors come from?
Light is one of the most mysterious of Earth's wonders. Find out what it is, how we see it, and how it can be used to make a better world.

LET THERE BE LIGHT!

Imagine you are looking out your window watching a powerful rainstorm at night. Then, without any warning—flash! The dark sky ripples with a lightning bolt. Seconds later, the rumbling of thunder fills the air. Boom! We've all seen it, but now let's learn what's behind that breathtaking display of sound and light.

A GIANT VIBRATION

Having just read the previous chapter, you might have guessed that something must be vibrating to cause thunder. After all, all sounds are caused by vibrations. If you thought this, then you are correct. Thunder is the result of lightning superheating the air and sending out vibrations that can be heard for miles. But why does the air vibrate and create such a loud noise? Electricity!

HOT LIGHT

Think of how you build up a static electric charge when you rub your sock-covered feet on a carpet. Clouds can build up large electrical charges too. Now think about how it feels when you touch a door handle and get zapped. In much the same way, a cloud's charge can travel through the air to the ground. When this happens, the air gets hot. REALLY hot. Over 20,000° Celsius! This super-heated air expands and then quickly cools off and collapses, clapping together, and causing the vibration that makes thunder.

But not only does the really hot air cause thunder, it is so hot that it glows. We call this glowing air lightning. And light is what this chapter is all about!

Candlelight is a very hot light.

I SAW THAT!

Light is a form of energy that our eyes can detect. Like sound, light travels in waves, so scientists describe light with terms like **wavelength** and **frequency**. You now know sound travels in compression waves but light travels differently. We learned that sound cannot be heard in the vacuum of outer space, but look up at the night sky and you will see the moon and the stars even though the vacuum of space separates us. Unlike sound, light **can** travel through a vacuum, which is why sunlight can reach us through outer space. Light is most commonly created by extreme heat. The sun and the wick of a burning candle are examples of objects that are so hot that they create light.

CASE STUDY: Turn on the Light

Almost all the light we use and enjoy comes straight from the sun. However, we all turn on lightbulbs every day to make life a lot brighter. Lightbulbs have changed a lot over time. There are lots of different types of lightbulb, but let's explore three popular ones.

1. The First Lightbulbs

The earliest type of lightbulbs are called incandescent (in-can-<u>des</u>-int) bulbs. The inventor Thomas Edison became rich and famous for perfecting this type of bulb. Incandescent bulbs have a thin piece of metal—thinner than a human hair—called a filament inside them. When electricity moves though the filament, it gets so hot that it creates light. However, a lot of energy is wasted as heat, making these bulbs somewhat inefficient. That is why they are being phased out today.

2. Compact Fluorescents

Do you use lightbulbs that look like swirly ice cream? They are compact fluorescent bulbs (CFLs), and they are replacing many incandescent bulbs. CFLs contain a gas that gives off light when electricity travels through it. CFLs make light without as much heat, and therefore, require much less energy. They also last a lot longer. People are so used to the shape of incandescent bulbs that many CFLs are now built to look like them. Early CFLs were dim when first turned on, but the technology is improving.

3. LEDs

Another way to make light is with a light emitting diode, called an L-E-D for short. LED lights are very tiny and are used in lots of different devices, such as TVs, remote controls, car dashboards, and study lamps. LEDs last longer and use less energy than all other types of electric light. They also come in all sorts of fun colors.

LIGHTEN UP!

Have you ever been in a situation where you wished you had a flashlight with you? There are some organisms that never have that problem because they have a structural adaptation which allows them to make their own light.

Instead of heat or electricity, these living things use chemicals inside them to make light. Their lights are used for many reasons, including attracting mates, hunting for prey, and confusing predators, but scientists are still puzzled about why a mushroom would need to glow. Can you think of a reason?

This scientist is studying glow-in-the-dark mushrooms in Brazil.

A firefly

An anglerfish

49

TALKING ABOUT LIGHT

We are so used to daylight that we don't give it much thought. We wake up and expect it to be light outside our windows. But stop for a moment and think about light. All light has a source. The sun is the main source of light you see outside during the day. What would life be like without the light of the sun? Earth would be a dark, cold, dreary place. There wouldn't even be moonlight, since the light of the moon is just sunlight reflecting off the moon's surface. Without light we would not even be here because our food sources—plants or animals that eat plants—depend on light from the sun.

Light travels from its source in straight lines called rays. The light you see outside has traveled from the sun to Earth in a direct path.

In this chapter, you are going to learn all about the properties of light: how it moves, how it bends, how it bounces off some objects, yet moves through others, and how it can be dispersed into different colors.

HOW FAST IS LIGHT?

When you walk into a dark room and turn on a light switch, the room seems to become light in an instant, but did you know that it actually takes time for the light to travel from the bulb to all parts of the room? The time is so incredibly short that we can't see it happening.

Light travels fast. Really, really, ***really*** fast. Faster than you are probably imagining. In fact, nothing in the universe is faster than light, which streaks along at 671 million miles an hour. It takes light 8 minutes and 20 seconds to go 93 million miles (or 150 million km) from the sun to Earth. A car zipping along nonstop at 100 km per hour would take over 170 years to travel the same distance!

Here's another way to think about how fast light travels. Light can travel around the Earth seven times in just one second. Light is about a million times faster than sound, which is why you will never hear thunder before you see lightning (unless the lightning is hidden by clouds).

It takes a lot of special equipment to stop light. Of course, when her equipment is in use, Dr. Hau always wears protective goggles to keep her safe.

SCIENTIST IN THE SPOTLIGHT: RACING WITH LIGHT

Never challenge light to a race because you will definitely lose, unless you get help from scientist Lene Hau. She led a team that used lasers and very, very cold equipment to slow down light to the speed of a bicycle! She and her team even stopped light completely. Why try to slow down light? It might help improve computers, communications, and night-vision goggles.

KEY WORDS TO KNOW

LIGHT
A form of energy that our eyes can detect.

REFLECTION
The bouncing of light off an object.

REFRACTION
The bending of light as it passes from one medium to another.

PRISM
An object that refracts and disperses white light into visible light.

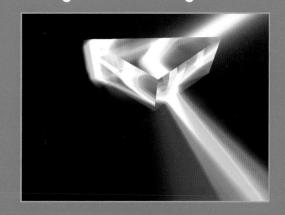

TRANSPARENT
Allowing light to pass through easily.

TRANSLUCENT
Allowing some light to pass through.

OPAQUE
Stopping light from passing through.

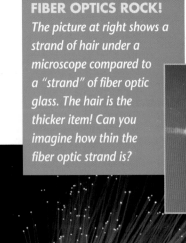

LIGHT WAVES

Light is a vital form of energy, and almost all living things depend on light energy to survive. Green plants need the energy in sunlight, or from artificial lights, to make their own food. They store light energy in their fruits, leaves, stems, and roots. All animals (including you) either eat plants or other animals that once ate plants to get that stored energy. When you chomp on an apple, you are biting into a tasty bundle of energy made possible by light.

THE POWER OF LIGHT

Most of the sunlight that hits Earth goes unused. What can we do to change that? Solar panels convert light energy into electrical energy, which can be used to charge your cell phone, music player, and even heat your home. Solar panels are good for the environment because they do not generate any pollution and are powered by a renewable resource—the sun.

TALKING WITH LIGHT WAVES

You might be surprised to learn that people use light every day to talk to each other, watch TV, and send information through the Internet. How? Fiber optics!

Grab a strand of your hair, prepare to say "ouch," and give a quick tug. See how thin that strand is? Now try to imagine a strand of glass that is one tenth the thickness of your strand of hair. You are now picturing a fiber optic cable.

These tiny glass cables are used to send information around the world. Your voice, your favorite TV shows, and all your e-mail messages are converted into pulses of light that can travel at blazing speed (remember how super-fast light is) through a network of fiber optic cables. Each individual fiber can carry ten million phone calls at the same time!

FIBER OPTICS ROCK!

The picture at right shows a strand of hair under a microscope compared to a "strand" of fiber optic glass. The hair is the thicker item! Can you imagine how thin the fiber optic strand is?

This photo shows light zooming through fiber optic wires.

LIGHT WAVES MADE SIMPLE

You've already read that light has a lot in common with sound because it travels like a wave, but there is one big difference. Light and sound move in different types of waves. Here's how to remember the difference: Stretch a Slinky loosely along the floor and give one end a push. You will see a wave move through the Slinky even though the Slinky stays in a straight line. This type of wave is called a **compression** or **longitudinal wave**. Sound waves travel in that way.

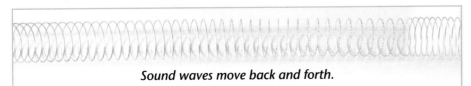

Sound waves move back and forth.

Now shake one end of the Slinky back and forth so it starts to make a snake-like pattern. This type of wave is called a **transverse wave**. Light waves travel this way.

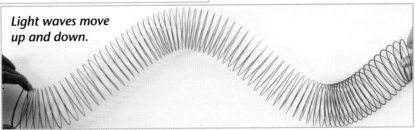

Light waves move up and down.

LIGHT'S WAVELENGTHS

Even though sound waves and light waves are different types of waves, scientists use some of the same vocabulary, such as **wavelength** and **frequency**, to describe both types of waves. A light wave has a top— the **crest**—and a bottom— the **trough** *(troff)*. Let's compare the two kinds.

Sound wave wavelength: the distance between two compressions or rarefactions

Light wave wavelength: the distance between two crests or two troughs in a wave.

You can also describe a wave by how many times it has a crest each second. This is called the wave's frequency. When the wavelength gets shorter, the frequency increases because there are more crests per second. When the wavelength gets longer, the frequency decreases.

wavelength

crest   crest

trough

Do you remember that sounds with short wavelengths and high frequencies are high-pitched, and sounds with long wavelengths and low frequencies are low-pitched? Light's wavelength and frequency are also very important. They are responsible for every glorious color you have ever seen.

Light wave with a long wavelength and low frequency.

Light wave with a short wavelength and high frequency.

53

There is something about a rainbow that makes us want to stop in our tracks and just stare.

SEEING COLOR

Every rainbow reveals a surprising fact. White light is a combination of several different wavelengths of light traveling together. The wavelength of light is what determines the color we are seeing. Red light has the longest wavelength and violet has the shortest wavelength. All the other colors have wavelengths in between.

OVER THE RAINBOW
Water droplets in the air separate light into its various wavelengths so we see each color distinctly.

ROSES ARE RED, VIOLETS ARE VIOLET

Look at this diagram. Notice that as you move from red to violet, each wavelength gets a little shorter. The diagram shows the visible spectrum—*the six main colors of light. Some people remember their order by putting the first letters of each color into the name ROY G. BV.*

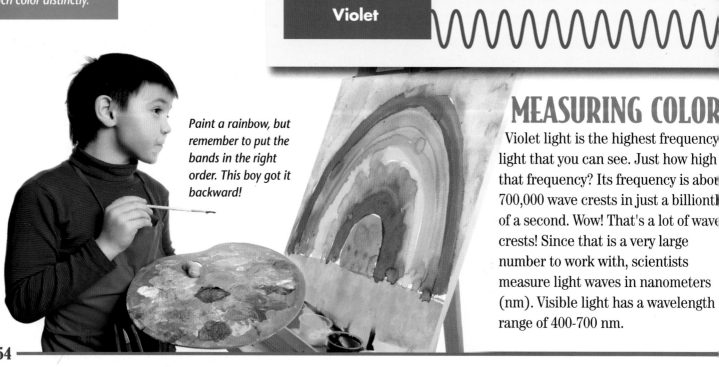

| Red |
| Orange |
| Yellow |
| Green |
| Blue |
| Violet |

Paint a rainbow, but remember to put the bands in the right order. This boy got it backward!

MEASURING COLOR

Violet light is the highest frequency light that you can see. Just how high that frequency? Its frequency is about 700,000 wave crests in just a billionth of a second. Wow! That's a lot of wave crests! Since that is a very large number to work with, scientists measure light waves in nanometers (nm). Visible light has a wavelength range of 400-700 nm.

WHY IS GRASS GREEN AND THE SKY BLUE?

"What's your favorite color?" is a question that only you can answer. "Why is that banana yellow?" is a question that science can answer. Remember that white light is a combination of all the colors of light. When light hits the banana, the banana absorbs all the wavelengths of light that are not yellow. The yellow wavelengths bounce off the banana (like a ball bouncing off the ground) into your eyes.

All the colors you see are made this way—different objects absorb different colors. Grass is green because grass mostly reflects only green light. Roses are red because roses mostly reflect only red light. Why is the sky blue? When sunlight moves through the sky, most of the longer wavelengths such as red and orange pass through with almost no scattering. However, much of the shorter wavelength light such as blue and violet gets scattered all around the sky. The scattered blue light travels to our eyes for us to see. Are you wondering what *color* light is that has a longer wavelength than red or a shorter wavelength than violet? None! There are light wavelengths that are longer or shorter, but we can't see them.

If we cannot see any other rays, how can we know they exist? Have you ever gotten a sunburn? Your eyes could not see this shorter wavelength, but skin is very sensitive to it. This wavelength—shorter than violet—is called ultraviolet and it is just one of many invisible rays.

MIXING COLOR

If you mix red, green, and blue paint together, you get a muddy, dark brown color. Light is very different. Mixing red, green, and blue light together creates white light. In fact, even if you mix all six colors of light together, you will still get white light.

WHAT ANIMALS SEE

Some creatures *can* see ultraviolet light. Spiders and bees are two critters that see things very differently than we do as a result. Compare the flower the way we see it and the way a bee might.

Other animals see the same things we do but with different colors. Let's compare this brightly attired pooch as seen through other animal eyes.

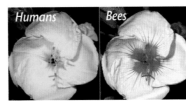

Humans   Bees

Squirrels see only blue and yellow.

Rabbits see only blue and green.

Cats and dogs see very muted colors.

INVISIBLE WAVES
UNSEEN BUT IMPORTANT

Just as there are some sounds that are too low or too high for our ears to detect, there are wavelengths of light that our eyes cannot see. These wavelengths of light are hugely important in our day-to-day lives.

The **visible spectrum**, the light that the human eye can see, represents a small part of a whole range of wavelengths of light energy. Scientists call the entire range of light the **electromagnetic spectrum**.

Sunlight has most of the entire electromagnetic spectrum. A little less than half of the sun's energy comes to us as visible light. Part of the sun's radiation is wavelengths longer than red light known as **infrared** *(in-fruh-red)*.

Other wavelengths that are even longer than infrared have familiar names: **microwaves** and **radio waves**. Microwave ovens send invisible waves that heat up food. Their wavelengths are too big to escape through the metal mesh that you see on the door of your microwave. Radio towers send invisible radio waves that are detected by your radio's antenna. Radio waves have wavelengths the length of a football field. Radio waves aren't sound. Radio speakers convert them into sound vibrations.

Waves that are shorter than violet include **ultraviolet (UV) rays**, **X-rays**, and **gamma rays**. These have tiny wavelengths, closer to the size of a teeny atom. UV rays can damage eyes and skin. Sunscreen and sunglasses help block harmful UV rays.

CASE STUDY:
The Wide World of Waves

Other light waves are important. We can't see them, but we can use many of them!

1. The Longest Waves
These rays are used to communicate over long distances or explore outer space. Also used by cell phones, and MRI machines that can safely scan inside your body.
WHAT ARE THEY? RADIO WAVES

2. Cooking/Chatting Waves
Use these rays to quickly heat up food. Cell phones also use these waves. WHAT ARE THEY? MICROWAVES

3. Hot Waves
The sun's warmth comes from these rays. Nightvision goggles use them. WHAT ARE THEY? INFRARED WAVES

4. Seeing Waves
These are the only rays human eyes can detect.
WHAT ARE THEY? VISIBLE LIGHT WAVES

5. Just Out of Sight Waves
What comes after ROY G. BV? These waves do. We can't see them, but bees and other insects can.
WHAT ARE THEY? ULTRAVIOLET (UV) RAYS

6. Probing Waves
These rays move through your soft-tissues but are absorbed by bones—ideal to see what's going on inside your body. WHAT ARE THEY? X-RAYS

7. The Shortest Waves
The most penetrating type of ray, these can cause illnesses such as skin cancer but can also be used to treat other cancers. WHAT ARE THEY? GAMMA RAYS

4. Visible color

1. Radio Waves   2. Microwaves   3. Infrared   5. Ultraviolet   6. X-rays   7. Gamma Rays

Length of each ray

A football field   YOU!   A bee   A pin-tip   A bacterium   A virus   A molecule   An atom   A nucleus

LASERS AND LIGHT

Have you ever gone to a sporting event and seen people "do the wave"? When people raise their hands and stand up at the same time in an organized way, it looks like a wave moving through the crowd. Light is normally not this organized. Light waves move in a more disorganized way.

A laser is a device that makes an intense ray of light Because laser light can be easily focused, it can be used for many purposes including running a CD player, performing surgery, and even cutting through metal.

USING RAYS TO HELP US SEE DIFFERENTLY

How can a doctor determine if you've broken a bone or a dentist look inside your teeth for cavities? How can an airport make sure that nothing dangerous is in someone's luggage? How can an art historian detect other sketches hidden beneath a painting? The answer is by using X-rays. These high frequency, short wavelengths of energy are invisible to our eyes but can penetrate right through most matter and be turned into pictures. So be careful and try not to break a bone, but know that if you do, an X-ray will help a doctor fix it.

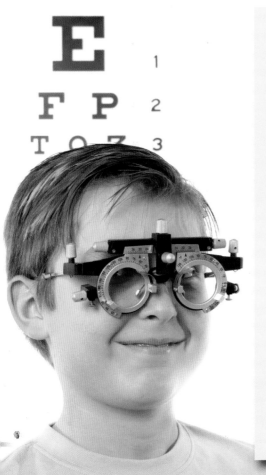

HOW YOUR BODY SEES LIGHT

You can read these words, but how do you actually see them? The dark circle in the middle of your eye is called a pupil, which is surrounded by the colorful iris. Your pupil controls how much light gets into your eye by expanding and contracting in diameter.

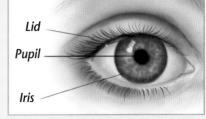

Light bounces off this page toward your eye. That light travels through a lens behind your pupil and hits your retina. Your retina sends a message through your optic nerve to your brain. Finally, your brain gets the message that a book is in front of you. It all happens super-fast!

Having two eyes allows you to see if objects are close or far away. Find a friend and try this: You'll need a paper cup and a coin. Put the cup on a table and stand about 3 to 4 meters away.

Cover one eye. Have your friend hold the coin at arm's length above the cup, but slightly in front of it. Keeping your eye on the coin, tell your friend when the penny is directly over the cup. Have your friend drop the penny. How close was it? Try it with the other eye, then both eyes. What happened?

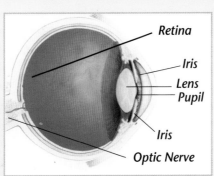

Who is that absolutely gorgeous person staring back at you in the mirror?

REFLECTION

Imagine playing a basketball game on a pumpkin patch. It would be very frustrating. Whenever you bounced the ball, it could go flying off in any direction. Basketball courts are flat so you can more accurately predict where a bouncing ball will go.

Like a ball, light can also bounce off the surfaces that it hits. Remember, light travels in a straight line until it encounters an object. Once the light hits an object, it can bounce off. We call this the bouncing of light off a surface a **reflection**. Like basketballs on a bumpy surface, the reflection of light is normally scattered in many random directions.

Most surfaces scatter light because they are much bumpier and more uneven than they look. You might think the paper of this book is smooth, but magnified, you would see that it is actually very rough.

This is a very magnified look at paper. Notice how lumpy it is!

FOLLOW THE BOUNCING LIGHT

If you were as small as a ray of light, the paper this book is printed on would seem more like a mountain range. The paper's surface is bumpy all over. When light rays hit it, they are reflected in many different directions. But some surfaces, such as a mirror or the surface of a pond, are so smooth that light rays bounce off them as perfectly as a basketball bouncing off a polished wood court.

Next time you bounce-pass a basketball to a friend, you can think of how similar that is to light bouncing off a mirror. When you stand in front of a mirror, light bounces off you and onto the mirror. Then some of it bounces back into your eyes, allowing you to see your reflection.

Light scatters
When light bounces on a bumpy surface, it scatters in many directions.

Light bounces
When light bounces on a smooth surface, it creates a perfect reflection.

PUTTING MIRRORS TO WORK FOR US

Most mirrors are made of polished glass with a thin coating of silver behind them. Light waves bounce off this polished surface without scattering. All the light that hits the mirror is reflected away equally. Of course, mirrors are useful for making sure we don't have food stuck in our teeth or checking to see that our hair looks good, but mirrors have many other very important uses.

Many types of cameras and telescopes work by using mirrors to reflect light. Searchlights use multiple mirrors to create more intense beams of light. Flashlights use curved mirrors to focus light beams. Dentists depend on mirrors to see those hard-to-see, way-back teeth, and rearview and side mirrors on cars make driving much safer. Can you think of any other useful mirrors?

MIRROR, MIRROR ON THE WALL
Go on a mirror hunt in your house. How many mirrors are there? Don't forget makeup mirrors, mirrors on baby toys, and those in pet cages.

MOON MIRROR
Did you know that astronauts left a mirror on the moon? Scientists can reflect lasers from Earth off this mirror to measure exactly how far away the moon is. They discovered that the moon is slowly moving away from Earth!

CASE STUDIES: Build a Periscope

A periscope is a simple tool that uses mirrors to see things that you would normally be unable to see. Submarines use periscopes to check out what's on the water's surface. Spies use them to peek around walls. How will you use yours? *Materials: 2 small mirrors, tape, scissors, and a tall, skinny milk carton.*

1. Cut two eye-holes in the box: one on the bottom side of the box and the other on top opposite side of the box. These are the holes that the light will reflect through.

2. Position a mirror at a 45° angle inside the box at each eye-hole. Make sure that the mirrors are facing each other: It's important that light from one mirror reflects onto the other mirror. Once the mirrors are in the right spot, tape them in the box.

3. Look through the bottom eye-hole. You should be able to see through the top eye-hole. If it doesn't work, try taping the mirrors in slightly different positions. Happy spying!

Spoon Science

You normally use flat mirrors, but curved mirrors can be really useful too. Let's investigate how reflections form on curved surfaces, using the humble spoon. *Materials: a shiny, metallic spoon.*

1. *Polish the spoon using a cloth (such a cotton shirt). The cleaner the spoon, the better your results will be.*

2. *Hold the spoon up to your face so you are looking at the inside of the spoon. Notice anything weird? Your reflection is upside down! This type of mirror is called a* **concave** *surface (it sinks in).*

3. *Flip the spoon over so you are looking at the back of the spoon. Your reflection is now right-side up. You also have a wider field of vision. This type of mirror is called a* **convex** *surface (it sticks out).*

Concave mirrors make objects look upside down because the light waves are reflected at different angles than flat or convex mirrors. Concave mirrors are used in car headlights and telescopes. Convex mirrors are used on vehicles' side-view mirrors and in buildings to see around corners.

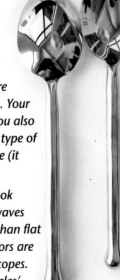

REFRACTION

Light sometimes goes right through an object. If this didn't happen, then you would not be able to see through a glass of water or a swimming pool. When light goes from one medium, such as air, into another medium, such as water, the light waves are bent. The bending of light waves as they pass from one medium to another is called **refraction**. Refraction happens because the speed of the light wave changes when it enters the new medium. Refraction explains why a spoon in a glass of water appears bent or broken, or why fish in a pond appear closer to the surface than they actually are!

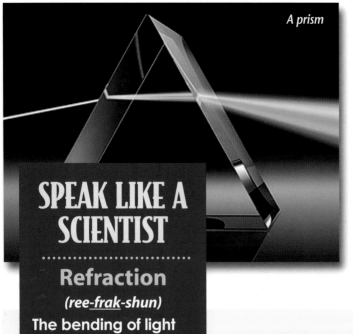

A prism

SPEAK LIKE A SCIENTIST

....

Refraction

(ree-*frak*-shun)

The bending of light as it passes from one medium to another.

BREAK IT UP, PRISM

A **prism** is a triangular wedge of glass or plastic. When light passes through a prism, the different wavelengths of visible light are refracted as they change speed and direction. Then the refracted light is separated or dispersed into its rainbow of colors. You see a rainbow because different wavelengths of light bend at different angles. For example, red light bends just a little and violet light bends a lot. In natural rainbows, raindrops act as little prisms and mirrors, refracting and reflecting white light from the sun and turning it into a rainbow.

DO YOU WEAR GLASSES?

The lenses in your eyes refract light onto your retina. If the light doesn't hit the retina just right, images will be blurry. Eyeglasses and contact lenses can help your vision. These lenses bend the light just the right amount so the light accurately hits your retina and you can easily focus on what you are looking at.

Can't see the writing on the blackboard? Some glasses help correct vision so we can see distances, using lenses that curve slightly inward. Are the letters in a book blurry? People who have trouble clearly seeing objects that are close to them need glasses with lenses that curve slightly outwards. Both kinds of eyeglasses work by using refraction.

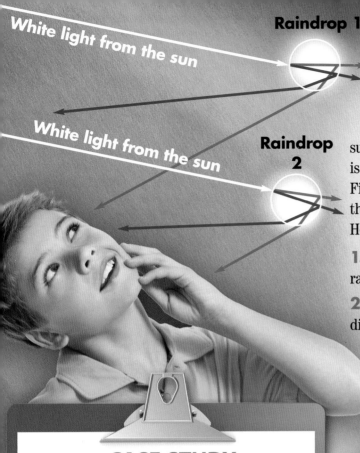

White light from the sun

Raindrop 1

White light from the sun

Raindrop 2

RAINBOWS: PRISMS OF WATER

Three things must happen for a natural rainbow to occur. First, it has to be raining. Second, the sun must be shining. This doesn't happen often because if it is raining near you, the sun is usually covered by clouds. Finally, you must be standing directly between the sun and the rain. Got all three things? Now you can see a rainbow! Here's what happens.

1. A white ray of sunlight passes through the round raindrop.

2. This white light gets separated into many colors. (This diagram only shows a purple and red ray for simplicity).

3. Some of the red and purple rays continue through the other side of the raindrop, but some of them reflect back out of the raindrop.

4. The red and purple rays bend even more when they exit the raindrop out of the same side that the white light enters.

5. Someone who is standing between the sun and the rain will see red rays from the high drops and purple rays from the lower drops. The raindrops in between create the orange, yellow, green, and blue of the rainbow.

CASE STUDY: Rainbow in a Glass

Next time it's a sunny day grab a glass of water and a piece of white paper. Not sunny? Use a flashlight instead.

1. Hold the glass of water between the paper and the sunshine or flashlight.

2. Carefully change the position of the glass and the angle that you are holding the paper. With patience you will catch a rainbow on your paper.

CONCLUSION: *The different wavelengths that make up sunlight are refracted and get separated from each other when they move through the water. Those different wavelengths hit the paper to reveal the colorful rainbow.*

CASE STUDY: Make a Magnifying Glass

The world's simplest magnifying glass! Materials: a piece of thin transparent plastic cut from a soda bottle (about 4 cm by 2 cm), water.

1. Put the plastic over something you want to magnify, such as any letter in this sentence.

2. Use your finger (or the tip of a pencil) to dab a water drop onto the plastic. Start with a water drop that's about 0.5 cm wide. Look at a letter beneath the drop. You might have to lift the plastic a little for better results. Do things look bigger?

The drop makes objects appear 5 to 10 times larger. It refracts the light as it passes through the curved surface of the water drop, making everything look bigger. Try different size water drops and compare.

OOOOOH! WHAT A BEAUTIFUL REFRACTION!

Sunsets produce a range of colors as light gets refracted through the air, changing from yellow to red, and even blue and purple.

TRANSPARENT

TRANSPARENT, TRANSLUCENT, AND OPAQUE

Pretend that you are a ray of light traveling through the air. You are about to bump into a pillow. You have a couple of choices to make. You could reflect off the pillow. You could pass through the pillow. You could let the pillow absorb your energy. You could even do any combination of the three choices. Obviously, light doesn't make choices; it obeys scientific laws. The way that light will react with something determines if the material is **transparent**, **opaque** *(oh-payk)*, or **translucent**.

CRYSTAL CLEAR

If you lived in a house that had windows made of bricks, it would be a very dark house. Windows are made of glass because glass is **transparent**, which means light passes through it easily. On the other hand, you'd never want to play hide-and-seek in a room full of transparent furniture—there would not be a place to hide! Clear glass, clean water, air, and clear plastics are transparent materials.

CLEAR AS MUD

If light does not pass through something, then that material is described as **opaque**. Most objects in your classroom, such as whiteboards, desks, and walls are opaque. You probably don't have to think hard about why you want your clothes to be opaque! Opaque objects such as mud, wood, brick, stone, concrete, and metal reflect and/or absorb all the light that hits them and do not allow light to pass though.

OPAQUE

BLURRED RAYS

You've probably noticed that there are some objects in your house that are not transparent, but they are also not opaque. In other words, you can kind of see through them, but not very well. Materials that let some light pass through them are **translucent**. Waxed paper, frosted glass, and tracing paper are some things that are translucent. Sunglasses use translucence to cut down on the light from the sun, and nature creates translucence with fog. Translucent materials provide some privacy without making things completely dark.

BLURRY WINDOWS AND FROSTY DOORS
Is there any frosted glass in your home? Your school? In shops or businesses in your community? Be on the lookout!

Transparent	Translucent	Opaque
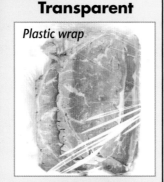 Plastic wrap	 Colored plastic bags	 Foil
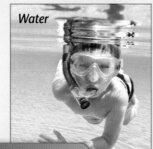 Water	 Tracing paper	 Bricks
 Glass jar	 Thin fabric	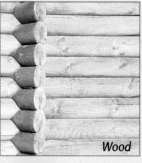 Wood
	Frosted glass	 Thick paper

CASE STUDY: A Sorting Scavenger Hunt

How many transparent, translucent, or opaque items are there in your classroom or home? Let your eyes be the judge!

1. *Gather a variety of different materials. Some suggestions: colored plastic lids, paper towel, waxed paper, aluminum foil, cardboard, plastic wrap, bubble wrap, cloth, and stained glass.*

2. *Hold each material against a dark wall and shine a flashlight on it, or you can hold it up to a light source or a sunny window.*

3. *Does any light pass through the material? Classify your materials according to their ability to block light. List the translucent materials from least translucent to most translucent.*

RECAP AND REVIEW

LIGHT

Light is a form of energy we can see.
Light travels in a straight line unless something gets in the way.

LIGHT IS REFLECTED...

...when it bounces off an object.

LIGHT IS REFRACTED...

...when a light wave is bent as it moves from one medium to another.

TRANSPARENT
Light passes through easily.

TRANSLUCENT
Light passes through partially.

OPAQUE
Light does not pass through.

Long wavelength

THE VISIBLE SPECTRUM
Wavelengths that the human eye can see.

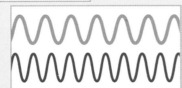

Short wavelength

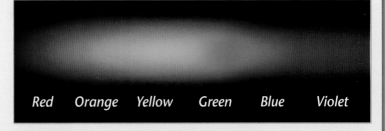

Red   Orange   Yellow   Green   Blue   Violet

Use pages 48-49 to answer questions 1 and 2.

1. What is light?

2. How is light most commonly created?

Use pages 50-51 to answer questions 3 and 4.

3. In what direction does light travel?

4. Why is lightning most often seen before thunder can be heard?

Use page 52-53 to answer questions 5 and 6.

5. Light travels using what type of wave?

6. Draw a diagram and label a representation of a light wave, including wavelength, crest, and trough.

Use pages 54-55 to answer questions 7 and 8.

7. Explain the relationship between wavelengths and the color of light that we see.

8. What are the colors of the visible spectrum?

Use pages 56-57 to answer question 9.

9. What is the visible spectrum?

Use pages 58-59 to answer questions 10 and 11.

10. Explain how light is reflected off a textured surface like sandpaper.

11. Explain how light is reflected off a smooth surface like a mirror.

Use pages 60-61 to answer questions 12-14.

12. Describe what happens to a ray of light when it goes from one medium to another. What is that called?

13. What happens to white light as it enters a prism?

14. Explain the relationship between the reflection and refraction of light and the formation of a rainbow.

Use pages 62-63 to answer question 15.

15. Copy and complete the chart below.

Word	What does the word mean?	List a material with this property.
Transparent		
Translucent		
Opaque		

YOU ARE THE SCIENTIST

When you look at a red sweater, you see red because the sweater is reflecting the red wavelengths while absorbing all the other colors' wavelengths. Keeping that thought in mind, on a hot summer day would you rather wear a white shirt or a black shirt? Explain why.

DATA DETECTIVE

Some people have difficulty telling the difference between certain colors. This graph shows the percentage of all men and all women who are "color-blind." What can you infer from this data?

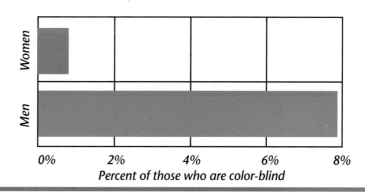

Percent of those who are color-blind

This photograph shows water two ways: A solid and a liquid. Water molecules can also exist as a gas. Are there any other chemicals that can exist in more than one state?

CHAPTER FOUR

WHY MATTER MATTERS

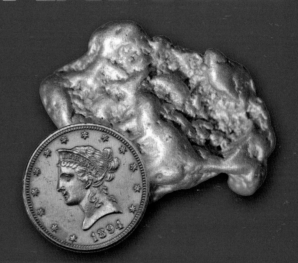

Gold is called an element. Unlike water, which is made of atoms of hydrogen AND oxygen, gold is only made of one kind of atom: gold.

Just a typical day in your kitchen—water boils on the stove, freezes into ice in your fridge, and quenches your thirst as a cool liquid straight from the tap. How can water do all that? What other things exist in nature that are capable of such great feats?

Explore an unseen world of whizzing, whirling particles and find the answers!

MATTER AND MASS

What do the shoes on your feet, a barnyard chicken, the ice cream you hope gets served for dessert tonight, a soccer ball, and your best friend have in common? They are all made of **matter**. Think of matter as a fancy word for "stuff." A cloud, a dirty fingernail, a fire station, and a glass of orange juice are also made of stuff and, therefore, are made of matter. Does this mean that everything is made of matter? Well, not exactly. Ideas and actions like curiosity, friendship, Tuesday, hiccups, and being polite are not made of matter because they are not objects. Every object, whether it is as microscopic as your DNA or as huge as our sun, is made of matter.

WEIGHING IN

A more formal definition of matter is anything that has mass and takes up space. If something has mass, it means that force will be required to change its speed or the direction of motion. Even if it is super-small—a raindrop, a speck of dust, or an ant's eyeball—it is still made of matter. **Mass** is the word we use to describe the *amount* of matter in an object.

People often confuse mass and weight but they are not the same. An elephant and a car both have more mass *and* weight than a hamster and a skateboard. The reason it is easier to lift a hamster than an elephant is because the hamster has less matter in it. Because it has less matter, it weighs less.

So what *is* the difference between mass and weight? Well, it all depends on where that elephant or hamster is in the universe!

MASS AND VOLUME

This balloon takes up more space than the brick and therefore has a greater volume. Volume is the amount of space that a solid, liquid, or gas occupies. But the brick has more mass than the balloon because it has a lot more matter in it. More matter means more mass. Size has nothing to do with mass. Ping-pong and golf balls have the same volume but different masses.

MASS OR WEIGHT

The amount of matter in you does not change if you go someplace else. If you have a mass of 40 kg on the Earth, you would still have a mass of 40 kg on the moon. There is still the same amount of stuff inside you. However, your *weight* would change. Weight is a measure of the gravitational pull on an object.

The greater the mass of a planet or moon, the greater its gravitational pull. The moon has only 1/6 the amount of Earth's gravity because the moon is less massive than the Earth. This means that everything on the moon weighs 1/6 of what it weighs on Earth. Forty kg is about the same as 90 pounds, so if you stepped on a bathroom scale on the moon, the scale would show just 15 pounds (90 ÷ 6 = 15).

Here's another way to think about it. Pretend that on Earth you are able to lift a 50-pound box. On the moon, you could lift six of these boxes at the same time!

Now let's blast over to Jupiter. You still have the same 40 kg of matter in your body. Your mass on Jupiter is the same as your mass on the Earth, but Jupiter is much more massive than the Earth. It has a stronger gravitational pull so everything weighs about 2.3 times as much on Jupiter. There, your 90 pounds on an Earth scale would jump to about 213 pounds. Of course Jupiter is made mostly of gas, so you can't exactly plop a bathroom scale down and hop on!

CASE STUDY: Space Scales

Hop on an imaginary scale on every planet in our solar system!
If a person weighing 90 pounds (about 40 kg) on Earth stepped on a scale on these planets the scale would read...

1. **Mercury**
   34 lbs (15 kg)
2. **Venus**
   82 lbs (37 kg)
3. **Our moon**
   15 lbs (7 kg)
4. **Mars**
   34 lbs (15 kg)
5. **Jupiter**
   213 lbs (97 kg)
6. **Saturn**
   96 lbs (44 kg)
7. **Uranus**
   80 lbs (36 kg)
8. **Neptune**
   101 lbs (46 kg)

SCALES IN SPACE
Using a spring scale could, in theory, record different weights on each planet, but a balance scale, which uses standards of fixed mass, would record the same mass everywhere. Why? Both the standards and the object being weighed are subject to the same gravitational forces.

SINK OR FLOAT?

If you drop a feather and a brick into a pond, why does the feather float and the brick sink? If you said it's because the brick is heavier, think about other things you've seen floating on water that are much heavier than feathers, such as an aircraft carrier—a ship that is so large that airplanes can land on it. An aircraft carrier is definitely a lot heavier than a brick. So how can that big boat float?

Even though an aircraft carrier is really heavy (it has a lot of matter in it), it is also really big (it takes up a lot of space). An object will float if its volume is large compared to its mass. A feather and an aircraft carrier do not have that much matter in them compared to their volume, so they float. A brick has a lot of mass compared to its volume, so it sinks.

THE LANGUAGE OF MATTER

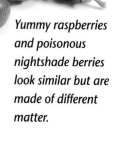

Take a look at the berries on the right. They are both bright red and about the same size. But one is a deadly posion. What makes that happen? It's all a matter of **matter**. If you want to discover why some plants are healthy to eat and some are poisonous, you need to understand what type of matter they are made of.

Every object in the universe is made of matter. That's why it is important to learn more about matter. Understanding matter can help explain our world. If you want to invent a better baseball bat, you need to know what type of matter or material to use. The reason glass is transparent and breakable and steel is opaque and strong is because they are made of different types of matter.

THE MYSTERIES OF MATTER

Hopefully you are getting curious about matter. After all, there are lots of different types out there. No matter what you are interested in—sports, music, animals, food, or the latest video game—it all comes down to the kinds of matter involved.

Scientists study matter by understanding **elements**, **compounds**, and **mixtures**. They also study matter's **phases—solid**, **liquid**, and **gas**. Once you understand these concepts, you will have a greater appreciation for the world and all the matter in it. Someday you might become a chemist and make a career out of studying matter, because there is a *lot* to explore.

Yummy raspberries and poisonous nightshade berries look similar but are made of different matter.

HANDLE WITH EXTREME CARE
This young scientist is visiting a medical lab where the dress code requires gloves, gown, safety glasses, and a hair cap.

Crocs and crocodiles—both are made of matter.

KEY WORDS TO KNOW

MATTER
Anything that has mass and takes up space.

ATOM
The smallest unit of an element.

ELEMENT
Matter made of only one type of atom.

C stands for carbon

MOLECULE
A combination of atoms bonded together. The smallest unit of a compound.

Molecules can be an element that bonds with the same element or different elements that link.

COMPOUND
A substance made of at least two different elements bonded together.

CO_2 is carbon dioxide.

MIXTURE
A combination of two or more substances that are not bonded and can be separated by physical methods.

Air is a mixture.

SOLUTION
A mixture in which one substance dissolves in another.

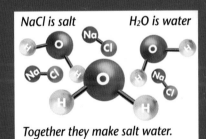

NaCl is salt H_2O is water

Together they make salt water.

SOLID
Molecules packed together so they hold their shape and do not flow.

LIQUID
Molecules that are loosely packed together and can flow past each other.

GAS
Molecules that move freely past each other with a lot of space between them.

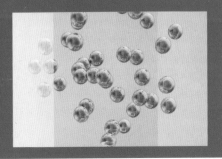

Small, smaller, smallest!

ATOMS

Element

Atom

Atom

Nucleus made of protons and neutrons

Electrons

Imagine that a teacher has a piece of gold and an amazingly sharp knife. She decides to cut the piece of gold in half. She then takes one of these smaller pieces and cuts *it* in half. She keeps repeating this step: Cutting a smaller piece in half, and then cutting the even smaller piece in half. Eventually, the piece would be too small for the knife to cut in half, but let's pretend that she had some other tool like a laser beam that could still cut the increasingly tiny piece of gold in half as she looked through a powerful microscope. Eventually, she would end up with one unbelievably tiny piece of gold. This extremely small piece of gold is called an **atom** of gold.

An atom is the smallest possible unit of an element. If you cut an atom of gold into two pieces, neither piece will be gold anymore. The word atom comes from an ancient Greek word that means indivisible or "un-cuttable." Nowadays, modern scientists have invented amazing ways to split atoms apart. Splitting an atom can release tremendous bursts of energy. That's how nuclear energy is made.

HOW SMALL CAN YOU GO?
A gold atom is the smallest bit of gold you can have that still has all the characteristics of gold.

LET'S GO ON AN ATOM HUNT!

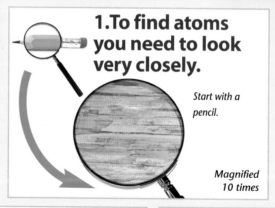

1. To find atoms you need to look very closely.

Start with a pencil.

Magnified 10 times

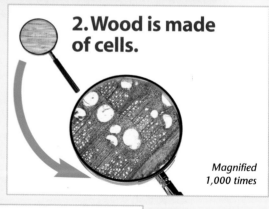

2. Wood is made of cells.

Magnified 1,000 times

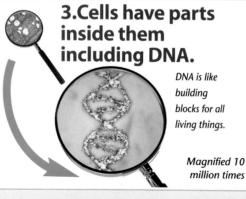

3. Cells have parts inside them including DNA.

DNA is like building blocks for all living things.

Magnified 10 million times

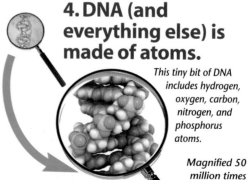

4. DNA (and everything else) is made of atoms.

This tiny bit of DNA includes hydrogen, oxygen, carbon, nitrogen, and phosphorus atoms.

Magnified 50 million times

When we look at things tinier than a cell, we often must use computerized images instead of actual photographs.

INSIDE AN ATOM

You might be asking yourself, "If all matter is made of atoms, then what are atoms made of?" Atoms are made of ultra-tiny bits called subatomic particles: **protons**, **neutrons**, and **electrons**.

All of an atom's protons and neutrons are packed tightly together in its center. This little bundle of protons and neutrons is called the **nucleus** (*new-klee-us*). Almost all the mass of an atom is located in its nucleus. Protons have a positive electrical charge and neutrons have no electrical charge.

An atom's electrons swirl around the outside of the nucleus—always moving. In fact, it's difficult to predict exactly where an electron will zip to next. Compared to protons and neutrons, electrons are very tiny and have very little mass. Electrons have a negative electrical charge, and it is the flow of electrons that creates electricity.

A NEW WAY TO LOOK AT ATOMS

Scientists once thought that electrons orbited a nucleus just like planets orbit the sun. You may still occasionally see diagrams with atoms drawn like this:

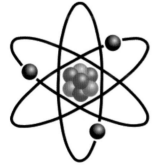

The old way to draw an atom

We now know that electrons can jump all over the place instead of staying in fixed orbits—behaving a bit like bugs swarming around a lightbulb on a dark summer night.

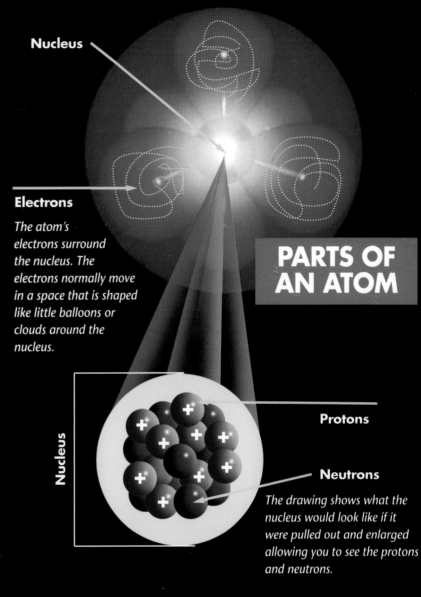

This is a computer-generated model of a neon atom. The nucleus is too small to be seen at this scale so it is represented by the flash of light at the center.

Nucleus

Electrons
The atom's electrons surround the nucleus. The electrons normally move in a space that is shaped like little balloons or clouds around the nucleus.

PARTS OF AN ATOM

Nucleus

Protons

Neutrons
The drawing shows what the nucleus would look like if it were pulled out and enlarged allowing you to see the protons and neutrons.

HOW BIG IS A NUCLEUS?

Imagine that an atom were somehow enlarged to be as big as a football stadium. The nucleus would still only be the size of a grape! The electrons would be the size of grains of sand and would often be in the farthest row of seats. Subatomic particles are very small and atoms are mostly empty space.

VOCABULARY ALERT!

Don't confuse the nucleus of an atom with the nucleus of a cell—something you'll learn more about in Chapter 5. The word nucleus in chemistry means something very different from the word nucleus in biology, just like a bat in the zoo is very different from a bat in a baseball game.

ELEMENTS

The ingredients for everything on Earth!

Suppose that you were in a big kitchen that had about 120 different ingredients such as eggs, sugar, flour, apples, salt, butter, pickles, chocolate chips, vegetable oil, and lemons. How many different recipes could you create? At first, you might think that you aren't a great cook and could only make a few different things. However, if you didn't mind experimenting a bit, you could make lots and lots of different creations by combining ingredients in many different ways.

By adding a little more of some ingredients and mixing them in different combinations, you could invent hundreds, thousands, even millions of different recipes. You could mix pickles with lemons! You could add more sugar or less salt. Yes, some would taste truly awful, but the point is that with only about 120 different ingredients, you could cook up an endless number of dishes.

Similarly, everything on this planet—leaves on trees, the air you breathe, tires on your bicycle, your favorite video game—are all made from about 120 different types of matter. How amazing! We call these basic types of matter **elements**.

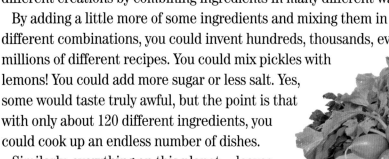

A RECIPE FOR EVERYTHING

Mixing different elements together is a lot like mixing lots of food ingredients together. The different combinations can produce yummy things or some things that are just plain "yuck."

BUILDING BLOCKS OF MATTER

When elements are arranged in different combinations, an infinite number of things can be created. You may already be familiar with the names of many elements such as gold, oxygen, carbon, aluminum, sodium, hydrogen, and nitrogen. Gold isn't made of anything except gold. Oxygen isn't made of anything except oxygen. You, however, are made of many different elements including oxygen, carbon, and hydrogen. There are also some elements that you have probably never heard of, such as antimony (used to make things fireproof) and germanium (used in fiber optic cables).

Just as a few ingredients can help you cook all sorts of delicious treats, when elements are combined, an almost infinite number of things can be created. Think about LEGO bricks. If you've ever played with LEGO bricks, you know you can combine these simple little rectangles into rockets, castles, or alien creatures. Now think of each different color of LEGO brick as a different element. Black might represent carbon, for example. Imagine that one black brick is an atom of carbon. Just as a stack of black bricks is made of only one color of brick, an element is a pure substance that is made of one type of atom.

Pretend that these black LEGO bricks are a hunk of the element carbon. Each brick represents one carbon atom.

THE TOP FIVE

Elements in your body

1. Oxygen
2. Carbon
3. Hydrogen
4. Nitrogen
5. Calcium

Elements in the Earth's Crust

1. Oxygen
2. Silicon
3. Aluminum
4. Iron
5. Calcium

Elements in our Galaxy

1. Hydrogen
2. Helium
3. Oxygen
4. Carbon
5. Neon

Look at these lists. Which elements appear on all three lists? Which have two in common? What can you infer from this?

ORGANIZING ELEMENTS

Take a good look at the table on the right (there is a larger version of it on the next page). It is one of the most famous tables in all of science, and you will keep seeing it all the way through college. Chemists depend on it. It is called the **periodic table of the elements**.

It lists all the elements there are. It also puts elements with similarities into groups. Each element has an abbreviation, called a chemical symbol. For example, H stands for hydrogen and O is for oxygen. Some symbols come from Latin names, so Pb stands for lead and Na means sodium. All elements also have a number, called their atomic number. The higher an element's atomic number, the more matter it contains. For example, gold (Au)—with an atomic number of 79—has more mass than aluminum (Al)—with an atomic number of 13. What are the atomic numbers for O and H? Look them up on the next pages and you'll know why they are both lighter than iron!

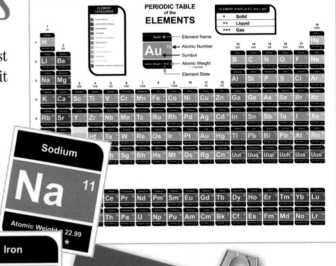

HOMEMADE ELEMENTS

All the elements with atomic numbers of 1 through 92 exist in nature. Elements greater than 92 are artificially made by scientists. Artificial elements (and a handful of natural elements) are normally very unstable—the technical word is "radioactive"—which means they easily fall apart into other simpler, naturally occurring elements. Scientists can create new elements by adding more protons to an atom's nucleus. If you create a new element, you get to help name it too!

CASE STUDY:
Iron for Breakfast

What do some rocks, blood, a nail, and many cereals have in common? They all have the element iron in them. Let's extract the iron from your breakfast! Materials: iron-fortified cereal (make sure "iron" is an ingredient—cornflakes work well), a really strong magnet, blender, a cup, shallow container, water, graduated cylinder.

1. Blend a cupful of cereal with 1 liter of water in a blender for 2 minutes. Pour your mixture into your container and let it sit for 5 minutes.

2. Slowly stir your magnet in the mixture for about 2 minutes. Pull out the magnet. You should see small black flecks of iron on the magnet!

Iron is an important nutrient that your body needs. Your blood uses iron to carry oxygen. Tiny pieces of iron are added to some cereals to improve nutrition.

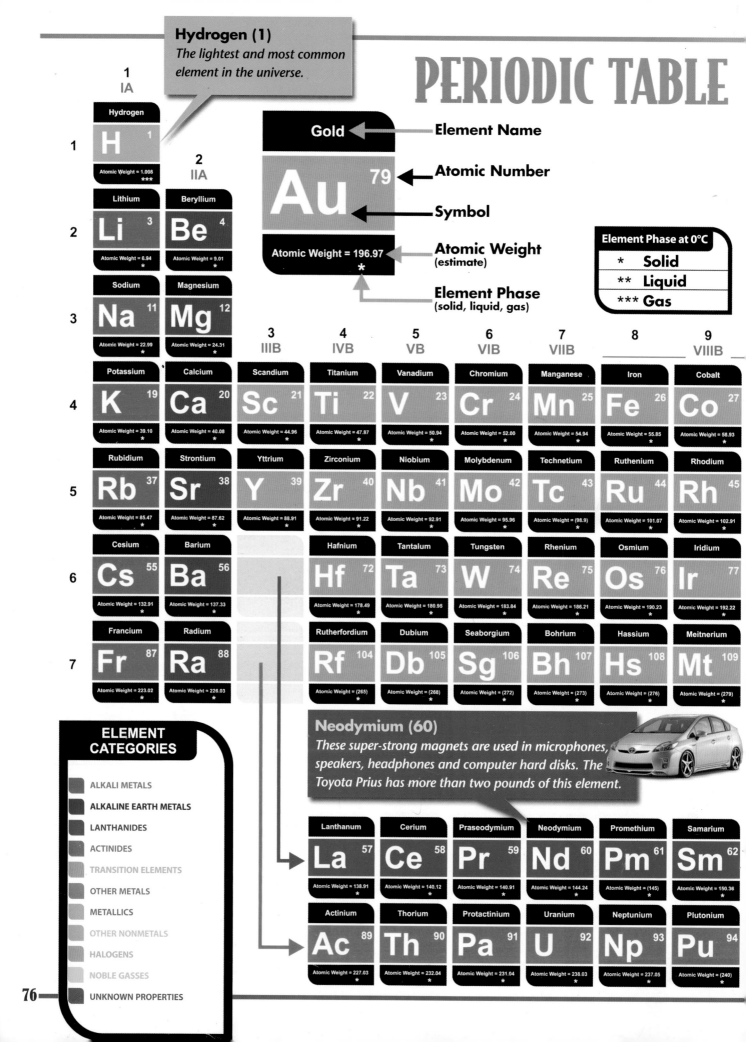

PERIODIC TABLE

OF THE ELEMENTS

Neon (10)
Used for glowing signs in store windows.

18
VIIIA

Hellium
He ²
Atomic Weight = 4.00
***

Carbon (6)
The "lead" in your pencil and diamonds are made of carbon atoms arranged in different ways.

Silicon (14)
Found in ordinary sand and used to make computers.

13 IIIA	14 IVA	15 VA	16 VIA	17 VIIA	
Boron	**Carbon**	**Nitrogen**	**Oxygen**	**Fluorine**	**Neon**
B ⁵	C ⁶	N ⁷	O ⁸	F ⁹	Ne ¹⁰
Atomic Weight = 10.81 *	Atomic Weight = 12.01 *	Atomic Weight = 14.01 ***	Atomic Weight = 16.00 ***	Atomic Weight = 19.00 ***	Atomic Weight = 20.18 ***
Aluminum	**Silicon**	**Phosphorus**	**Sulfur**	**Chlorine**	**Argon**
Al ¹³	Si ¹⁴	P ¹⁵	S ¹⁶	Cl ¹⁷	Ar ¹⁸
Atomic Weight = 26.98 *	Atomic Weight = 28.09 *	Atomic Weight = 30.97 *	Atomic Weight = 32.07 *	Atomic Weight = 35.45 ***	Atomic Weight = 39.95 ***

10	11 IB	12 IIB					
Nickel	**Copper**	**Zinc**	**Gallium**	**Germanium**	**Arsenic**	**Selenium**	**Bromine**	**Krypton**
Ni ²⁸	Cu ²⁹	Zn ³⁰	Ga ³¹	Ge ³²	As ³³	Se ³⁴	Br ³⁵	Kr ³⁶
Atomic Weight = 58.69 *	Atomic Weight = 63.55 *	Atomic Weight = 65.38 *	Atomic Weight = 69.72 *	Atomic Weight = 72.64 *	Atomic Weight = 74.92 *	Atomic Weight = 78.96 *	Atomic Weight = 79.90 **	Atomic Weight = 83.80 ***
Palladium	**Silver**	**Cadmium**	**Indium**	**Tin**	**Antimony**	**Tellurium**	**Iodine**	**Xenon**
Pd ⁴⁶	Ag ⁴⁷	Cd ⁴⁸	In ⁴⁹	Sn ⁵⁰	Sb ⁵¹	Te ⁵²	I ⁵³	Xe ⁵⁴
Atomic Weight = 106.42 *	Atomic Weight = 107.87 *	Atomic Weight = 112.41 *	Atomic Weight = 114.82 *	Atomic Weight = 118.71 *	Atomic Weight = 121.76 *	Atomic Weight = 127.60 *	Atomic Weight = 126.90 *	Atomic Weight = 131.29 ***
Platinum	**Gold**	**Mercury**	**Thallium**	**Lead**	**Bismuth**	**Polonium**	**Astatine**	**Radon**
Pt ⁷⁸	Au ⁷⁹	Hg ⁸⁰	Tl ⁸¹	Pb ⁸²	Bi ⁸³	Po ⁸⁴	At ⁸⁵	Rn ⁸⁶
Atomic Weight = 195.08 *	Atomic Weight = 196.97 *	Atomic Weight = 200.59 **	Atomic Weight = 204.38 *	Atomic Weight = 207.20 *	Atomic Weight = 208.98 *	Atomic Weight = (209) *	Atomic Weight = (210) *	Atomic Weight = (222) ***
Darmstadtium	**Roentgenium**	**Copernicium**	**Ununtrium**	**Ununquadium**	**Ununpentium**	**Ununhexium**	**Ununseptium**	**Ununoctium**
Ds ¹¹⁰	Rg ¹¹¹	Cn ¹¹²	Uut ¹¹³	Juq ¹¹⁴	Uup ¹¹⁵	Uuh ¹¹⁶	Jus ¹¹⁷	Uuo ¹¹⁸
Atomic Weight = (278) *	Atomic Weight = (283) *	Atomic Weight = (285) *	Atomic Weight = (287) *	Atomic Weight = (289) *	Atomic Weight = (291) *	Atomic Weight = (293) *	Atomic Weight = (295) *	Atomic Weight = (294) *

Curium (96)
This glows in the dark and is named after Marie Curie, a brilliant scientist.

Aluminum (13)
How would we make aluminum foil without this?

Iodine (53)
Gives seaweed a distinctive taste and smell.

Europium	**Gadolinium**	**Terbium**	**Dysprosium**	**Holmium**	**Erbium**	**Thulium**	**Ytterbium**	**Lutetium**
Eu ⁶³	Gd ⁶⁴	Tb ⁶⁵	Dy ⁶⁶	Ho ⁶⁷	Er ⁶⁸	Tm ⁶⁹	Yb ⁷⁰	Lu ⁷¹
Atomic Weight = 152.97 *	Atomic Weight = 157.25 *	Atomic Weight = 158.93 *	Atomic Weight = 162.50 *	Atomic Weight = 164.93 *	Atomic Weight = 167.26 *	Atomic Weight = 168.93 *	Atomic Weight = 173.04 *	Atomic Weight = 174.97 *
Americium	**Curium**	**Berkelium**	**Californium**	**Einsteinium**	**Fermium**	**Mendelevium**	**Nobelium**	**Lawrencium**
Am ⁹⁵	Cm ⁹⁶	Bk ⁹⁷	Cf ⁹⁸	Es ⁹⁹	Fm ¹⁰⁰	Md ¹⁰¹	No ¹⁰²	Lr ¹⁰³
Atomic Weight = 243.06 *	Atomic Weight = (247) *	Atomic Weight = (248) *	Atomic Weight = (251) *	Atomic Weight = 252.08 *	Atomic Weight = 257.10 *	Atomic Weight = (257) *	Atomic Weight = 259.10 *	Atomic Weight = 162.11 *

GAS, LIQUID, SOLID

Matter can exist in three different forms.

Think about these three things: ice cubes in a glass of lemonade, raindrops falling from a cloud, and the steam from a hot shower. They don't seem like they have much in common, but ice, raindrops, and steam are all forms of exactly the same thing—water. Matter, including water, can exist in several different forms called **phases**. The three basic phases of matter generally found on Earth are solids, liquids, and gases. What makes each phase special is how the individual molecules of matter are arranged.

LOOSE LIQUIDS

If you magnified a drop of water, you would see that the molecules of water are not just vibrating: They are also moving around a lot! This difference in molecule motion is a distinct phase—**liquid**. Liquids have a definite volume but do not have a definite shape. For example, one liter of water could either fill up a tall, skinny container or a short, wide container. The water adjusts or conforms to whatever shape surrounds it. However, there is still only one liter of water in either container. The volume has not changed.

STIFF SOLIDS

It's easy to swish your hand through a bucket of water, but impossible through a bucket of solid ice. The molecules of water in the ice are very hard because they are organized into a crystal-like pattern that gives it strength. When matter is packed together like ice, it is called a **solid**. Solids have a definite shape and volume. For example, an ice cube will stay the same shape and size as long as it stays cold. But here is a "cool" fact. If you magnify a piece of ice with a special microscope, you will see that the molecules of water are staying in the same place, but are vibrating. Their vibrations are just much too tiny to see with your eyes or feel with your hands.

ENERGETIC GASES

If you magnified steam, you would see that the molecules of water are bumping into and whizzing past each other with great speed. In fact, the molecules in steam are not even hanging out together (like in a solid or liquid), but are really far apart. This distinction leads to our final phase: **gases**. Gases have no definite shape and no definite volume. A gas will not only conform to fill any shape that holds it, but if you make the shape even larger, the gas will expand to fill the new spaces.

CHANGING PHASES

What makes matter change phase? One answer is temperature. Let's start with a solid. As you heat it up, the solid's molecules gain energy. These excited molecules start to lose their tight grip on each other and eventually start moving around. The solid has now melted into a liquid. As you increase the temperature, the molecules start to move faster and faster. If it gets hot enough, the molecules in the liquid break away from each other completely and the liquid boils into a gas. If you cool a gas or liquid, the reverse happens.

Helium is a gas.

IT'S JUST A PHASE

What do phases have to do with the different elements? If you look back at the periodic table, you will notice that almost all of the elements are solids when the temperature is at or above 0°C. Almost all of these solid elements are metals such as tin, iron, silver, and platinum. Almost a dozen of the elements are gases at this temperature, such as hydrogen, oxygen, nitrogen, and krypton. Only two elements are liquids: mercury and bromine.

If you want to turn most solid elements into a liquid or gas, you need to add a lot of heat. To make liquid gold soup, you'd have to heat the element gold (Au) to 1,000°C. If you kept heating it to 3,000°C, you could make a golden gas!

Sulphur is a smelly solid. It is also one of the most useful elements on Earth. It's used in tire-making, road-building, and in growing crops.

Mercury is a liquid metal and very toxic. It must be used with extreme care and only by people trained to handle this element.

Oobleck behaves like a liquid but is also a solid.

CASE STUDY: Making Oobleck

Oobleck is a material that is not quite a solid and not quite a liquid. It's easy to make and fun to play with!

Materials: 0.25 liters of water • 1–1.5 cups (60-125 grams) cornstarch • large mixing bowl • food coloring

1. Put the water in the mixing bowl. Start adding one handful of cornstarch at a time and mix it into the water. You can use a spoon, but it's more fun to use your hands.

2. Keep adding handfuls of cornstarch, slowing down how much cornstarch you add until the mixture (called Oobleck) becomes a very thick liquid that is almost solid. You can always add more water if you make it too thick.

3. Add a few drops of food coloring if you want. You will notice that if you squeeze or push the Oobleck, it will be firm and feel like a solid, but if you just let it rest in your hand, it will flow like a liquid!

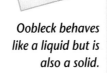

What happens when atoms hang out with other atoms?

MOLECULES

An atom can exist alone, but usually atoms are bonded (or stuck) to other atoms. When two or more atoms are bonded together they are called a **molecule**. Molecules can be simple or very complicated. A molecule of water is two atoms of hydrogen bonded to one atom of oxygen. The air you breathe contains oxygen molecules which are two atoms of oxygen bonded together. Pretty simple. On the other hand, a molecule of baking soda has six atoms in it and a sugar molecule has over three dozen atoms! Molecules can contain atoms from the same element or atoms from different elements. Your DNA—a combination of matter that is unique to your body—is a molecule made of billions of atoms bonded together.

HOW TO MODEL MATTER

Because molecules are so tiny, scientists often build models to understand them better. A common type of model is called a "ball-and-stick" model. Each ball represents one atom, and the balls are color coded to represent different elements. Carbon is always black. Oxygen is always red. Hydrogen is always white. Sticks are used to bond (connect) atoms together. Some models are really complicated!

Drawing pictures is another way scientists work with molecules. This drawing shows vitamin B3.

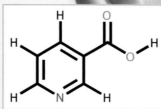

MAPPING MOLECULES

Atoms look like round spheres, so scientists often draw diagrams of molecules by using a circle with the element's chemical symbol inside it. Here are diagrams of four different molecules: water, carbon dioxide, vitamin C, and ozone. Can you count how many elements are in each? How many atoms are in each?

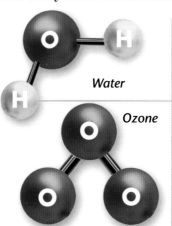

Water

Ozone

Carbon Dioxide

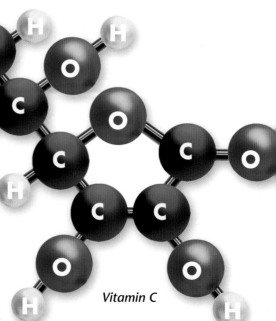

Vitamin C

*Answers: Water: 2 elements (oxygen and hydrogen), 3 atoms.
Ozone: 1 element (oxygen), 3 atoms.
Carbon dioxide: 2 elements (carbon and oxygen), 3 atoms.
Vitamin C: 3 elements (oxygen, carbon, and hydrogen), 20 atoms.*

CHEMICAL FREE?

Have you ever seen something in the grocery store advertised as "chemical free"? For this to be true, there must be absolutely nothing inside the box—not even air!

A chemical is simply a specific type of matter. Those advertisers are just talking about chemicals that might harm you, but there are plenty of healthy chemicals too. Salt is a chemical; water is a chemical; sugar is a chemical. All soaps, shampoos, and medicines are made of chemicals. Everything you eat, from your breakfast cereal to your dinnertime dessert, is made of chemicals. Even YOU are made entirely of chemicals. All matter is made from chemicals, so you can't have a "chemical free" anything.

NO CHEMICALS ADDED?
This girl's pasta sauce made that claim on its label. But now you know the entire jar was filled with chemicals!

CASE STUDY:
Invent your own molecule

Find some materials that you will pretend are atoms of different elements. For example, ball-and-stick models, LEGO bricks*, candy, or clay and toothpicks.

The different colors of the materials you choose will represent different elements.

1. *Most chemists have agreed to use certain colors to represent particular elements. For example, white represents hydrogen, red=oxygen, blue=nitrogen, and black=carbon. If you don't have these colors, make up your own color code. Just be sure to write it down like a good scientist!*

2. *Each single piece of your material will represent one atom of that element. One black LEGO brick is one atom of carbon. One red block is an oxygen atom. A white block represents a hydrogen atom.*

3. *Begin by building models of each of the molecules on the facing page to get the hang of it.*

4. *Now, join atoms together to invent a new molecule. Give your molecule a name. Make up some properties about your molecule. What might it be used for or what can it do?*

5. *Analyze your molecule. How many different elements are in it? How many atoms are in it? Swap with a partner and see if your partner agrees with your answer.*

In reality, only certain elements can combine to form molecules. Think about whether your make-believe molecule could occur naturally. For example, gold and silver would never bond together in nature.

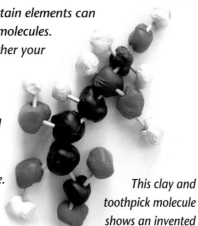

This clay and toothpick molecule shows an invented vitamin.

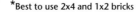

*Best to use 2x4 and 1x2 bricks

Let's "bond" over our love of compounds.

COMPOUNDS

SPEAK LIKE A SCIENTIST

Compound
A substance made of at least two different elements bonded together.

You breathe all the time because your body needs oxygen. Oxygen is an element—something made of only one kind of atom. But in nature, two atoms of oxygen are usually stuck together to form a molecule—two or more atoms that have bonded. Think of it as being like identical twins holding hands.

Although some molecules are made of only one type of element, most molecules are combinations of two or more different elements. A **compound** is any molecule made of two or more different kinds of elements bonded together. All compounds are made of molecules, but not all molecules are compounds. A molecule can be made from only one element. For example, O_2 is an oxygen molecule made of two oxygen atoms. However, *almost* all molecules are compounds. People often describe a molecule as the smallest unit of a compound.

Certain atoms snuggle up to the same kind of atom. Twinsies!

LET'S HANG OUT

There are some things in life that go really well together, like peanut butter and jelly, chips and salsa, or socks and shoes. Elements also bond together to make great combinations called compounds.

One of the most famous compounds is a simple one—two hydrogen atoms bonded to one oxygen atom. Think about the chemical symbols of these elements: two H's and one O. Another way to say this is H_2O. Sound familiar? It's water!

Sodium + Chlorine   react to form   salt!

CALLING ALL COMPOUNDS

Compounds are very different than the elements in them. You can combine two dangerous elements and end up with something totally harmless. Take the element chlorine. Chlorine is a poisonous green gas. It was used in World War I as a chemical weapon to harm enemy soldiers. Sodium is a soft, chalk-like metal that can explode if it gets wet. But when sodium and chlorine are combined, they form one of the simplest and most common compounds in the world—salt! Lucky for you and your french fries, salt will definitely not explode if it gets wet, nor is it green and poisonous, unlike the elements that make it.

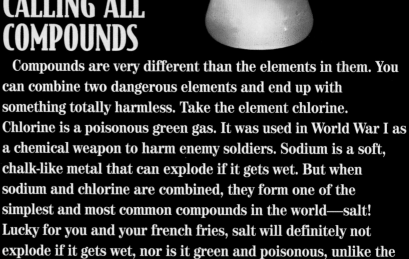

DESCRIBING MATTER

Pretend that four of your friends are having an argument about what water is made of. One friend says that water is made of elements. Another says that water is made of atoms. The third friend says that water is a compound. The fourth says it's a molecule. Who's right? Everyone!

1. Like all matter, water is made of elements. There are two elements in water—hydrogen and oxygen.

2. Water is made of atoms. Each molecule of water is made of three atoms— two atoms of hydrogen and one atom of oxygen.

3. Water is a compound. Water is a chemical made of two or more different elements, which also makes it a compound.

4. Water is a molecule. Water is a combination of atoms that have bonded together.

CASE STUDY: Making and Modeling a Compound

When chemicals react to form new compounds, the atoms rearrange themselves into a new combination. Let's turn some oxygen and iron into the compound rust.

Materials: fine steel wool, water, 2-3 teaspoons salt, plastic cup

1. *Fill the cup with water and dissolve some salt (salt speeds up the formation of rust).*

2. *Add the steel wool to the cup so the wool gets wet. Wait a day or two for the rust to form. While you wait for the rust, you can model the chemical reaction.*

3. *Find some materials (ball-and-stick models, LEGO bricks, candy, or clay) that you will pretend are atoms of different elements. The different colors of your materials represent different elements. Decide which element each color will represent.*

4. *Create four atoms of iron. Iron is written as Fe. Steel wool is mostly made of iron.*

5. *Create three molecules of oxygen. The oxygen comes from the water and is in the form O_2: two atoms of oxygen bonded together.*

6. *Break apart the oxygen molecules and connect them with the iron atoms to form two molecules of rust. Each molecule of rust should have two iron atoms and three oxygen atoms.*

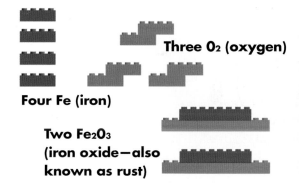

Three O_2 (oxygen)

Four Fe (iron)

Two Fe_2O_3 (iron oxide—also known as rust)

The chemical formula for rust is Fe_2O_3.

7. *After two days observe the rust that has formed on the steel wool. What happened?*

TASTE THE COMPOUNDS

Since we all have to eat to survive, the compounds we munch on are particularly interesting to learn about. Many sodas, teas, and coffee contain the compound caffeine, a stimulant that can keep you awake. Spicy foods get their kick from the compound capsaicin, a chemical that produces a burning sensation on your tongue. Caffeine and capsaicin are both made of four elements (hydrogen, carbon, oxygen, and nitrogen) but these compounds are unique because they use different amounts of these elements and arrange them in a different order.

Hot peppers can sizzle when you bite because of the arrangement of elements.

No need to feel mixed-up about...

MIXTURES AND SOLUTIONS

You might peek in the fridge and classify the food in it as being simple (an apple) or complicated (a seven-layer cake). Matter can be simple or complicated too. All matter can be classified as being either a **pure substance** or a **mixture**. A pure substance is matter that is made of either the same element or the same molecule. Every element is a pure substance.

Compounds such as salt are also pure substances. Salt is simply made of salt molecules (one sodium atom bonded to one chlorine atom). Sugar and carbon dioxide are also pure substances. Sugar is made of sugar molecules, and carbon dioxide has only carbon dioxide molecules in it. That's why they are called pure substances. There is nothing extra added to them. That's it, pure and simple.

MIX IT UP!

Although you probably use pure substances every day, they are not nearly as common as mixtures. Wood is not made out of molecules of wood, and dogs are not made out of tiny molecules of dog. Wood and dogs are mixtures made of many different types of chemicals.

A **mixture** is a combination of two or more substances that do not lose their identifying characteristics when combined. What does that mean? A mixture's different types of molecules still act the way they normally would if they were all by themselves. For example, if you pour some salt and sugar on a spoon you will have a mixture. If you taste this mixture, you will still taste the saltiness and the sweetness.

The air we breathe is a mixture of mostly nitrogen, oxygen, argon, carbon dioxide, neon, helium, methane, krypton, hydrogen, and xenon.

HOW WELL IS IT MIXED?

Scientists sort mixtures into two groups. Imagine filling a bowl with some peanuts and sesame seeds. Now shake it up. The larger peanuts will settle near the top and the smaller sesame seeds will tend to settle near the bottom. Not all parts of this mixture are identical. That's one kind of mixture.

A second type of mixture is blended so well that all the parts of the mixture are basically the same. For example, if you stir some sugar into a cup of hot water, the sugar water on the top of the glass will be as sweet as the sugar water on the bottom of the glass. All drops of this mixture are the same. Unlike the peanut and sesame seed mixture, you cannot pluck out the grains of sugar.

IS IT A PURE SUBSTANCE OR A MIXTURE?

All Matter

Pure Substances

Mixtures

Elements	Compounds	Slightly mixed	Completely mixed

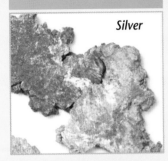

Silver

Salt

Grains of instant coffee dissolve completely in hot water.

JUST ADD WATER AND STIR

You probably are familiar with the word "solution." It means the answer to a problem. In chemistry, a **solution** means something very different. Solutions are mixtures in which one substance completely dissolves in another substance. For example, if you dissolve some salt in some water, you now have a solution of salt water.

You probably think that the water you drink is a pure substance and not a solution, but unless you are drinking distilled water, you are drinking a solution. Tap water and bottled water are solutions of water and small amounts of minerals. Solutions are everywhere!

CASE STUDY:
Separating a mixture

You've accidentally dumped some salt into a cup of sand. Can you get all the salt out? Let's try! You'll need: salt, sand, 2 cups, water, stirring spoon, measuring spoons, and a coffee filter.

1. Pour a teaspoon of salt and a tablespoon of sand into your cup. Mix it so it seems impossible to separate. You now have a mixture.

2. Pour some water into the cup until it's almost full.

3. Stir the mixture in the water until the salt dissolves. Now, you have made a solution of salt water that's also mixed with sand.

4. Pour the mixture onto a coffee filter over another cup. The salt water will drip through the filter while the sand stays on top.

5. The sand is now separated from the salt. Leave the salt water in a warm place. After a few days the water will evaporate, leaving behind salt. You have unmixed your mixture and separated your solution!

RECAP AND REVIEW

MATTER

Anything that has mass and volume

The mass of an object does not change, but its weight can change depending on the amount of gravity in its environment.

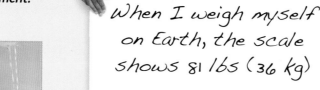

When I weigh myself on Earth, the scale shows 81 lbs (36 kg)

On the moon, the scale shows 13 lbs (6 kg)

MATTER CHARACTERISTICS

Gas
Takes the shape of a container, no definite volume, can be compressed, flows easily

Liquid
Takes the shape of a container, has a definite volume, not easy to compress, flows easily

Solid
Keeps a fixed shape, has a definite volume, not easy to compress, does not flow easily

As temperatures rise, matter changes from a solid, to a liquid, to a gas.

As temperatures drop, matter changes from a gas, to a liquid, to a solid.

REMEMBER THESE TERMS

Atom
The smallest part of an element.

Element
Substances that cannot be broken down any further; all matter consists of elements. Examples: H, O, He, C, Na, K

Carbon

Carbon Dioxide

Molecule
The smallest part of a substance that consists of two or more atoms.

Salt

Compound
Two or more combined elements that create a new substance. Examples: H_2O, NaCl.

Mixture
A combination of two or more substances where each substance keeps its own identity.

Solution
A mixture in which one substance dissolves in the other.

Use pages 68-69 to answer questions 1 and 2.
1. What is matter?
2. Explain the difference between mass and volume.

Use pages 70-71 to answer question 3.
3. Into what three phases do scientists classify matter?

Use pages 72-73 to answer question 4.
4. Sketch a model of an atom and label the nucleus, protons, neutrons, and electrons.

Use pages 74-75 to answer question 5.
5. What is an element? How do scientists list all the elements?

Use pages 78-79 to answer question 6.
6. Compare and contrast the characteristics of gases, liquids, and solids.

Use pages 80-81 to answer question 7.
7. What is a molecule? How do scientists create models of molecules?

Use pages 82-83 to answer questions 8 and 9.
8. What is a compound?
9. The diagram to the right shows the compound glucose (simple sugar). Use the diagram to determine how many carbon, hydrogen, and oxygen atoms are needed to create glucose.

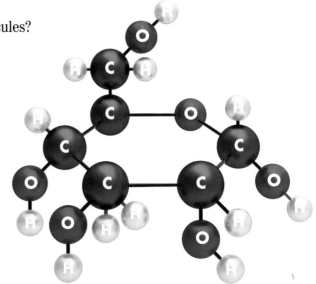

Use pages 84-85 to answer questions 10-12.
10. Explain the difference between a mixture and a solution.
11. What are two examples of a mixture?
12. What are two examples of a solution?

YOU ARE THE SCIENTIST

Design an experiment to explain how a change in temperature affects the phases of matter. Your design should include how the information will be recorded, what measurements will be made, what materials you will use, and how your data will be organized.

DATA DETETCTIVE What are three inferences you can make from the data?

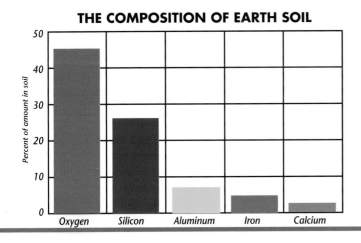

THE COMPOSITION OF EARTH SOIL

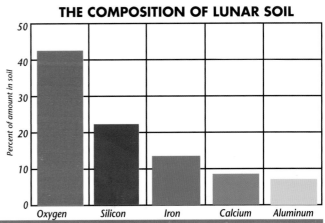

THE COMPOSITION OF LUNAR SOIL

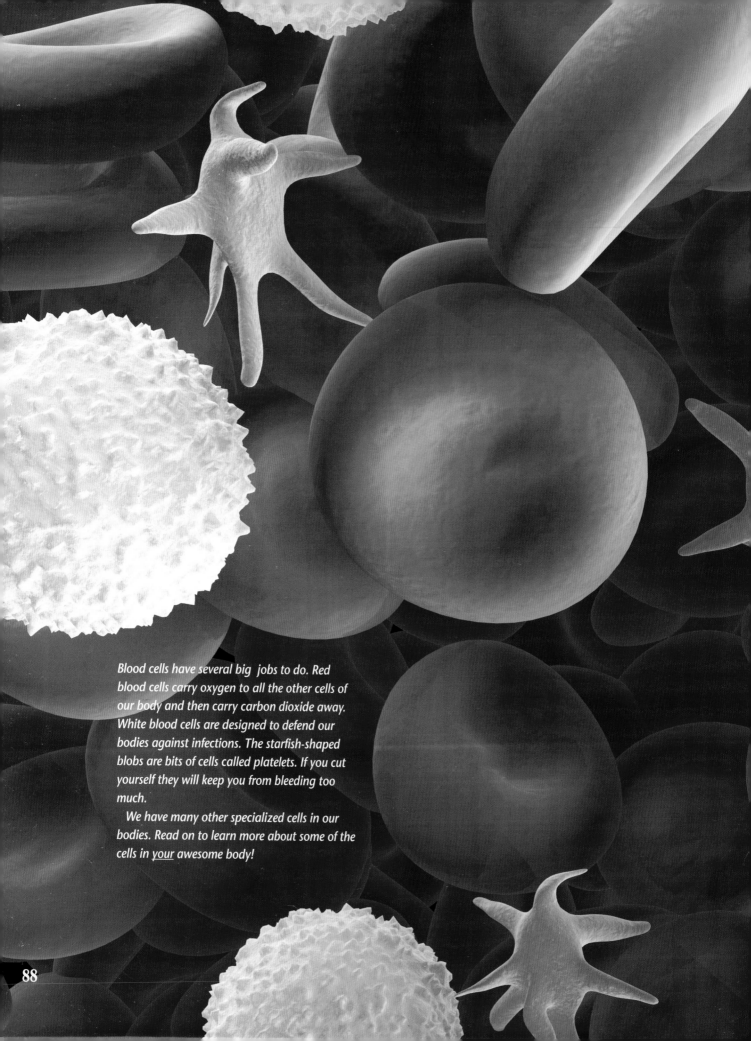

Blood cells have several big jobs to do. Red blood cells carry oxygen to all the other cells of our body and then carry carbon dioxide away. White blood cells are designed to defend our bodies against infections. The starfish-shaped blobs are bits of cells called platelets. If you cut yourself they will keep you from bleeding too much.

We have many other specialized cells in our bodies. Read on to learn more about some of the cells in <u>your</u> awesome body!

CHAPTER FIVE

CELLS AND ORGANISMS

Look closely at these blood cells. They look very different from one another, don't they? A human body has more than 60 TRILLION different cells. If you somehow could line up all your cells end-to-end, they would circle the Earth more than four times!

Let's peer more closely and discover what makes cells the building blocks of life.

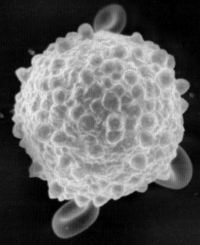

THE SECRET WORLD OF CELLS

Psssssst! Do you want to know the secret? You are not just you!

You are a colony of over 60 TRILLION microscopic living things that work together and depend on one another for survival. You are an amazing, organized, and very complicated collection of cells, and each cell in your body is alive!

THE LIFE OF A CELL

Cells are the tiny building blocks of life. Just as a book is made of pages and a house might be made of bricks, all living things are made of cells. Cells are the smallest unit of life. The cells in your body need food and oxygen, make waste, and respond to changes around them.

Because your cells are alive, it means they can die. You might be startled to learn that millions of your cells die every hour. But no need to worry! Your body is always making new cells to keep your body healthy and growing. Cells can reproduce themselves, constantly making new copies to replace the dying ones. There are more cells in your body today than there were yesterday. The number of cells in your body will continue to grow until you become an adult. When you are an adult, your body will keep your overall number of cells basically the same, replacing most of the ones that die with new ones.

One of the most amazing features of a cell is its ability to make copies of itself. The one cell seen below is splitting in half after duplicating its contents, to turn itself into two new cells.

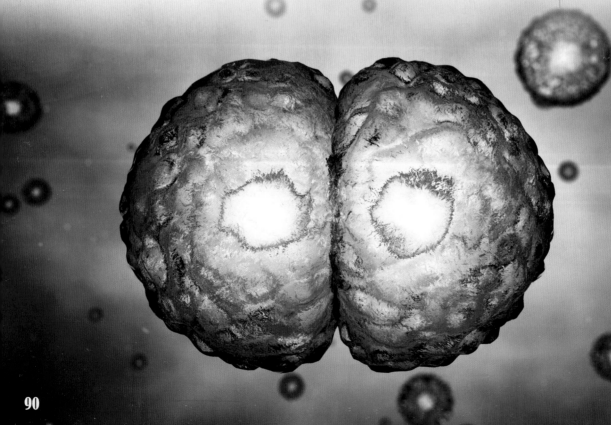

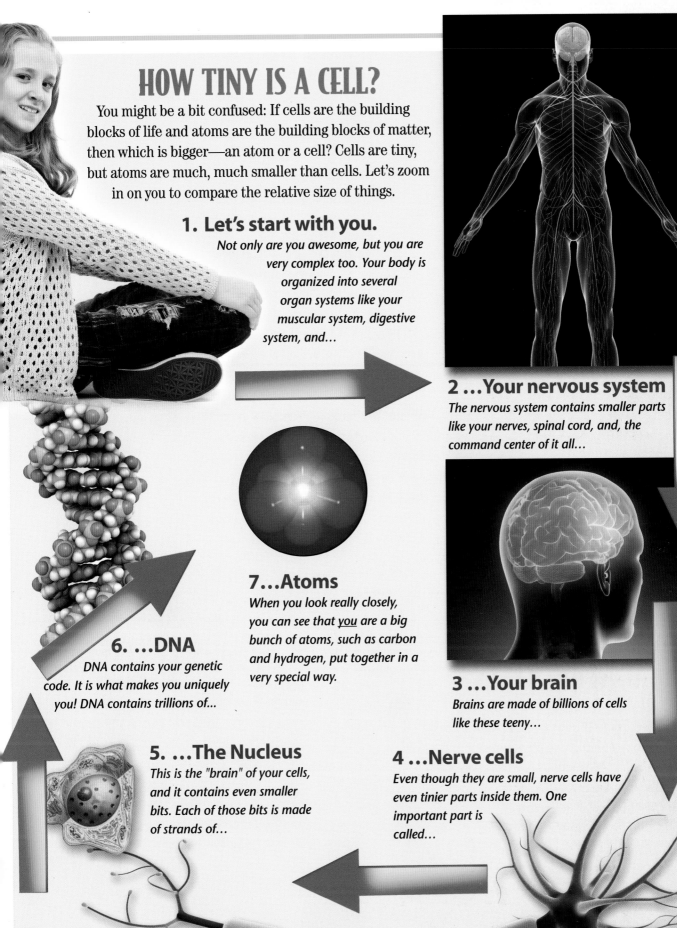

HOW TINY IS A CELL?

You might be a bit confused: If cells are the building blocks of life and atoms are the building blocks of matter, then which is bigger—an atom or a cell? Cells are tiny, but atoms are much, much smaller than cells. Let's zoom in on you to compare the relative size of things.

1. Let's start with you.

Not only are you awesome, but you are very complex too. Your body is organized into several organ systems like your muscular system, digestive system, and…

2 …Your nervous system

The nervous system contains smaller parts like your nerves, spinal cord, and, the command center of it all…

7…Atoms

When you look really closely, you can see that <u>you</u> are a big bunch of atoms, such as carbon and hydrogen, put together in a very special way.

6. …DNA

DNA contains your genetic code. It is what makes you uniquely you! DNA contains trillions of…

3 …Your brain

Brains are made of billions of cells like these teeny…

5. …The Nucleus

This is the "brain" of your cells, and it contains even smaller bits. Each of those bits is made of strands of…

4 …Nerve cells

Even though they are small, nerve cells have even tinier parts inside them. One important part is called…

LET'S TALK ABOUT CELLS

A "slice" of skin cells

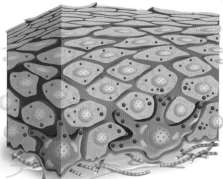

Think about the town in which you live and the people who work there. There are lots of different jobs being done by police officers, engineers, veterinarians, teachers, plumbers, and so many more. Your body is a lot like a town. There are hundreds of different types of cells in your body and each type of cell has a special job. By working together, these cells take care of one another, and therefore, you! Let's look at just a few of these living members of your body.

SKIN CELLS

Your skin cells group together to form a living armor that protects your body and also produces vitamin D. Your skin is composed of multiple layers of skin cells, and your outermost layer of skin is actually dead cells. Every day millions of these dead cells flake off and blow away without you even knowing!

BONE CELLS

The bones in a museum are dead and dry, but the bones in your body are very much alive. If you didn't have any bones, you'd be a shapeless blob. Some of your bone cells are very hard, while others are soft and spongy. When you break a bone, your bone cells remove the damaged cells and new bone cells fill in the break. Eventually, the new bone is as strong as it was before it was broken.

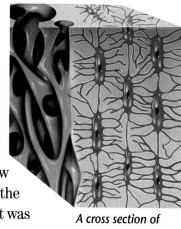

A cross section of bone cells

NERVE CELLS

The nerve cells in your brain and other parts of your body are like a complex and interconnected computer network. Nerve cells use chemical and electrical signals to send and store information. The longest cells in your body are nerve cells, some of which stretch from your feet to your spine!

A single nerve cell

MUSCLE CELLS

Without muscles cells, your body couldn't move. When you flex a muscle, the muscle cells contract and pull your tendons and bones along with them. Some muscle cells are controlled by your brain, while other muscles work on their own, pushing food through your digestive system and blood cells through your arteries.

A bundle of muscle cells

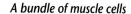

KEY CELL WORDS TO KNOW

These images will give you a better understanding of the functions of these cell-related structures.

ORGANISM
Any living thing, such as a plant, animal, fungus, yeast, or bacterium.

CELL
The smallest unit of life. Some organisms are made of just one cell. Others are made of many cells.

This is a bone cell.

HERE ARE SOME IMPORTANT PARTS OF A CELL. LET'S COMPARE THEM TO A SCHOOL.

NUCLEUS
(new-klee-us)

The control center of the cell. It holds the organism's DNA.

Think of it as the principal's office where all the plans for the school are kept.

CYTOPLASM
(sy-toe-plaz-um)

The fluid inside a cell.

Think of it as the air in a school, surrounding everything and everyone in the building.

CELL MEMBRANE
The outside layer of a cell that controls what goes in and out of the cell.
Think of it as a very floppy version of the walls, windows, and doors of a school.

VACUOLE
(vac-you-ole)

The part of a cell that stores food, water, and waste.

Think of it as a refrigerator and the trash cans in a school.

PLANT CELLS HAVE SOME ADDITIONAL PARTS.

CHLOROPLAST
(klor-oh-plast)

A plant cell part where photosynthesis happens, using sunlight to convert air and water into sugar.

Think of it as the school cafeteria.

CELL WALL
A thick, strong layer that runs outside the membrane of a plant cell that provides extra support.

Think of it as a brick wall or fence around the outside of a school.

PLANT AND ANIMAL CELLS

Humans, hermit crabs, and houseflies are obviously different from pine trees, pears, and pond lilies. However, when you look at animals and plants under a microscope, you see that they are remarkably similar. Not only are all animals and plants made of cells, but their cells have many of the same structures and parts—called **organelles** *(or-gah-nelz)*—inside them. Let's zoom in on a typical animal cell and plant cell to discover more.

THE CONTROL CENTER

The **nucleus** is the control center found in both animal and plant cells. The nucleus is like the computer (or brain) of a cell and holds all the information about what the cell should do. Your genes and a plant's genes are located in the nucleus and are coded as DNA. Genes are the reason you might have brown eyes, or freckles, or curly hair.

CELL SOUP

You've probably heard that you are mostly made of water. That's because the cells in your body are mostly made of a watery substance. Animal and plant cells are filled with a Jell-O-like substance called **cytoplasm**. Cytoplasm is full of helpful chemicals for the cell to use, and because the cytoplasm is a liquid, those chemicals can easily move to different parts of the cell.

FOUR IMPORTANT CELL PARTS

STORAGE CENTERS

You probably keep a lot of food and drinks in your refrigerator. Cells need to store food and water also, so they put them in tiny bubbles called **vacuoles**. Unlike your refrigerator, vacuoles are also used to store waste. Although both animal and plant cells have vacuoles, the plant cell vacuole is much larger. When a plant does not get enough water, the vacuole shrinks and the plant wilts. Next time you water a wilted plant, think about how you are refilling the vacuoles.

THE GATEKEEPER

Want to get inside a cell? Then you have to go through the **cell membrane**. The membrane is like the skin of the cell, yet it can open itself up to allow food in and let waste out. Both animal and plant cells have membranes, which protect the cell from unwanted intruders.

CROWDED CELLS

It helps to start learning about cells with simple diagrams, but simplified diagrams tend to make cells look rather empty. The truth is that cells are packed full of organelles and molecules. This drawing by David Goodsell, a molecular biologist who finds great beauty in cells, shows how crowded a cell can be. This is his drawing of an E. coli bacterial cell. As you can see, bacteria do not have a nucleus and they do not have their parts organized into organelles.

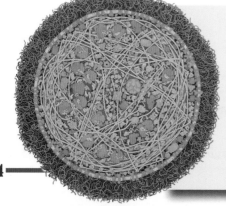

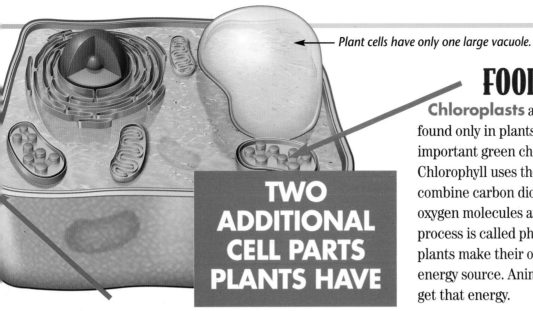

Plant cells have only one large vacuole.

TWO ADDITIONAL CELL PARTS PLANTS HAVE

FOOD MAKERS

Chloroplasts are an important cell part found only in plants. Chloroplasts contain an important green chemical called chlorophyll. Chlorophyll uses the energy of the sun to combine carbon dioxide with water to make oxygen molecules and sugar molecules. This process is called photosynthesis, which is how plants make their own food. The sugar is a cell's energy source. Animals must eat plant cells to get that energy.

NATURAL BRICKS

nts can't easily move around, so it's helpful
em to have some extra protection. Plant
have a **cell wall**, a layer that surrounds
embrane to provide more support. Cell
walls are the reason that plants
are often very sturdy and can
grow so tall.

CASE STUDY: Jell-O Cells

*aterials: 2 small zip-top plastic bags • 4-5 raisins
Four Jell-O cups or other gelatin • 4-5 green
rapes or cucumber slices • 20 pieces dried rigatoni
r other pasta • 2 cherry tomatoes • 1 large
rune or small plum • waterproof pen • 1 smaller
astic sandwich bag*

. Label the first zip-top bag as an animal cell. The
ag represents the animal cell membrane.
. Fill the bag part way with the gelatin mixture.
his is the cytoplasm.
. Add 1 cherry tomato to represent the nucleus.
. Add a few raisins to represent vacuoles.
. Take the second zip-top bag and label it a plant
ll. Using the smaller plastic bag (plant membrane),
peat steps 2 and 3 but use a prune instead of
aisins. Add grapes or cucumber (chloroplasts) and
al the bag. Place it in the zip-top bag.
. Add dried pasta pieces for the cell wall. Zip the
uter bag, then arrange the "cell wall" neatly to
rotect" the cell organelles. Use your super-sized cell
odels to remember important cell parts!

DO YOU WANT TO LEARN MORE?

There's a lot more in a school than just a principal's office and some doors, walls, and windows. In much the same way, a cell is a lot more than just a nucleus, a vacuole, cytoplasm, and a cell membrane. You'll learn more about a cell's other organelles in future years of biology. What? You can't wait? Then let's explore a few more important organelles.

Schools get energy from electrical outlets but cells cannot plug themselves into a wall. Instead, cells use their own internal power stations called **mitochondria** to extract energy from their food. These organelles are tiny; some cells contain thousands!

The principal has a plan for how the school should run, but the principal needs teachers to carry out the plan and share information with students. In a similar way, a cell has **ribosomes** where the instructions from the nucleus are used to make long chains of useful chemicals called proteins.

A school has a staff room where teachers can make photocopies and prepare lessons. A cell has a slightly similar part called the **endoplasmic reticulum** (or the ER). Some ER are packaging systems where many ribosomes make proteins. Other ER stores chemicals. The ER surrounds the nucleus. Some parts of the ER look like blankets folded back and forth (you can see it in both cell diagrams on these pages), and other parts look like a bunch of tubes.

A school has a custodian who helps keep things clean. In a cell **lysosomes** recycle waste and help digest food into more useful forms for the cell.

STUDYING CELLS

One of the very first people to see a cell was an English scientist named Robert Hooke. Hooke built a homemade microscope and in 1665, while studying a piece of cork, he saw the remains of the plant's cell walls. He grabbed a pen and paper and made the first sketches of cells ever drawn and decided the little chambers reminded him of the tiny rooms (called cells) where monks lived and prayed.

Hooke called these little objects cells and the name stuck. He had discovered that living (or once living) organisms are made up of much smaller, microscopic units or parts.

MICROSCOPES ROCK!

By refracting light, microscopes make objects look larger and open your eyes to new worlds.

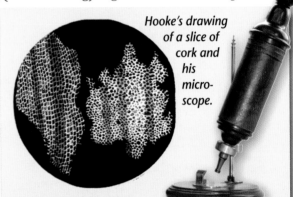

Hooke's drawing of a slice of cork and his microscope.

Magnified about 40 times

CASE STUDY:
Zooming in on Cells

Microscopes work best on thin objects. Because onion layers are very thin, they are excellent to view with a microscope.

Materials: microscope • onion • 2 plastic slides iodine • 2 cover slips • eyedropper • swab

1. *Peel apart an onion, and look for a very thin, clear layer that coats the thicker parts. Carefully peel off a small piece no larger than a fingernail.*

2. *Place the onion skin flat on the plastic slide.*

3. *Place a small drop of iodine on the onion skin. Be careful! Iodine is a strong stain and is toxic if swallowed.*

Human cheek cell

Nucleus
Cytoplasm

Cell membrane

Magnified about 400 times

4. *Wait 3 minutes for the iodine to stain the cells. (If you didn't add it, the onion cells would be too transparent to see very well.)*

5. *Gently place a cover slip over the stained onion skin, then look at your onion skin under the microscope. If possible, investigate what you can see with different magnification settings. What organelles can you see? Is your slide like the picture on the left?*

6. *You can also use a cotton swab to gently scrape some cells from the inside of your cheek (don't worry—you have millions). Repeat steps 2–5, then view.*

7. *Draw and label a picture of the cells you have seen.*

Cytoplasm   Cell wall

Nucleus

Vacuole

Magnified about 100 times

Cell membrane

Onion cell

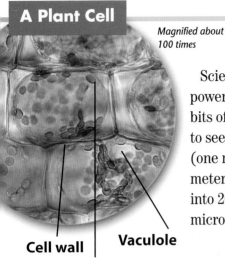

Magnified about 100 times

Cell wall | **Vaculole**

Chloroplast

ZOOMING IN

Scientists depend on extremely powerful microscopes to reveal the tiniest bits of cells. These microscopes allow us to see things as small as 500 nanometers (one nanometer is one *billionth* of a meter). That's the size of one hair divided into 200 strands. There are even special microscopes that can "see" a single atom.

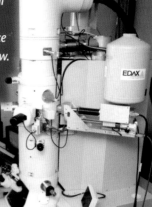

Electron microscopes are super-powerful and can show amazing detail like the yeast cell below. Can you see the nucleus?

Magnified about 1,000 times

WHAT YOU HAVE IN COMMON WITH A PLANT

You've seen that plant and animal cells have many of the same parts inside them. But hopefully you also noticed a few differences. What parts do plant cells have, that animal cells don't? Think about it first, then check the diagram below to see if you were right!

Plant Cells

- Cell wall
- Chloroplasts
- Large central vacuole
- Often square or box shape
- Make their own food

Both

- Cytoplasm
- Nucleus
- Cell membrane
- Vacuole

Animal Cells

- Small vacuoles
- Can be any shape, often a sphere
- Cannot make their own food

SCIENTIST IN THE SPOTLIGHT: ZAPPING KILLER CELLS

rmal body cells grow and divide and also know when to stop growing d die. Sometimes, cells become abnormal and grow and divide out of ntrol. This abnormal, speedy growth is called cancer, and it can be adly to the organism where it grows. There are many different types of cer. Rafael Davalos, a professor at Virginia Tech–Wake Forest School Biomedical Engineering and Sciences, won an award for curing a rador retriever of cancer. His cancer treatment used electricity to poke tiny holes in the cerous cells' membranes, which killed the cancerous cells. Scientists have found treatments some cancers, but not for all. Maybe someday <u>you</u> will discover a cure!

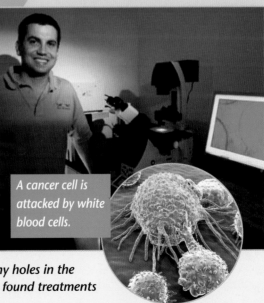

A cancer cell is attacked by white blood cells.

Magnified about 1,000 times

ORGANISMS

All living things are called organisms. Nobody knows how many different types of organisms or species live on the Earth. Scientists have found and named over a million of them, but they also think there could be many more millions of organisms that we just don't know about. Some of these unknown organisms dwell in the deepest parts of the oceans. Others live deep underground. And some just might live in your own body!

ONE OR MANY?

Organisms are either made of one cell or many cells. Single-celled organisms are called unicellular organisms. Because they are only one cell, unicellular organisms tend to be very small and you normally need a microscope to see them. Other organisms are made of many cells and are called multicellular organisms. All plants and animals are multicellular organisms.

CASE STUDY:
Two Unicellular Organisms

Meet two single-celled beings that could not be more different.

1. Lactobacillus

You cannot feel them and they are too small to be seen, but there are lots of friendly creatures living in your gut!

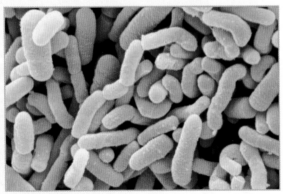

Yes, some bacteria can actually be good for you. These single-celled organisms help you digest your food and absorb nutrients. They even act like microscopic police, protecting you from other bacteria that might make you sick. Let's hear it for these little guys!

2. Caulerpa

Because this seaweed can grow over three feet tall, you'd probably think that it is made of many cells.

A caulerpa seaweed appears to have leaves, stems, and roots, just like a plant. But looks can be deceiving. Caulerpa is a green algae. It has just one cell with many nuclei. Think of that the next time you see it in a fish tank!

KEY ORGANISM WORDS TO KNOW

UNICELLULAR
(you-ni-sel-you-ler)

Made of only one cell.

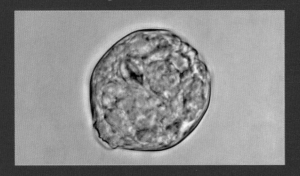

MULTICELLULAR
(mull-ti-sel-you-ler)

Made of more than one cell.

VERTEBRATE
(ver-ti-brate)

An animal with a backbone.

INVERTEBRATE
(in-ver-ti-brate)

An animal without a backbone.

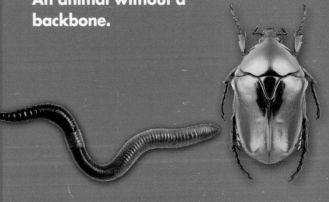

VASCULAR PLANT
(vas-kew-lur)

A plant with a system to transport water and food to its cells.

NONVASCULAR PLANT
(non-vas-kew-lur)

A plant without a system to transport water and food to its cells.

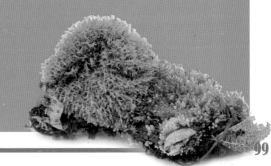

What do you share in common with an owl and a lizard?

VERTEBRATES AND INVERTEBRATES

A sea anemone

Study this picture of a sea anemone, an organism that lives in the ocean. It certainly looks like a plant, but the sea anemone has much more in common with you than with plants. That's because, just like you, the sea anemone is an animal. You might say that it doesn't move, so it must be a plant. But locomotion is not what makes plants and animals different. Besides, some anemones CAN move with a suction-like foot. Remember: The big difference between plants and animals is that plants make their own food, and animals must eat other things to get energy. Sea anemones eat small fish and shrimp, using their tentacles to sting their prey and sweep them into their mouth. Plants use the sun's energy to turn oxygen and carbon dioxide into sugar through photosynthesis. The oxygen plants make is used by animals to breathe, and plants are the food source for many animals.

GOT A BACKBONE?

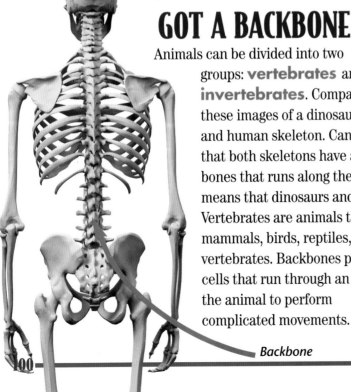

Backbone

Animals can be divided into two groups: **vertebrates** and **invertebrates**. Compare these images of a dinosaur and human skeleton. Can you see that both skeletons have a very long line of bones that runs along the back? This backbone means that dinosaurs and humans are vertebrates. Vertebrates are animals that have backbones. All mammals, birds, reptiles, amphibians, and fish are vertebrates. Backbones protect important nerve cells that run through an animal's body, allowing the animal to perform complicated movements.

Backbone

ANCIENT VERTEBRATES
Dinosaurs were the largest vertebrates to ever walk on Earth.

MEET SOME VERTEBRATES

Fish

Mammals

Birds

Amphibians

Reptiles

CASE STUDY:
The Red Panda

Red pandas live in China, Nepal, and Myanmar. They are much smaller than black-and-white pandas. They only grow to be about the size of a house cat. They live in trees and have long, furry tails they can wrap around themselves to keep warm. Though they are obviously vertebrates, scientists have had great difficulty classifying them, because they are similar to pandas but also to raccoons. So for now, they are classified into their very own group.

The more details scientists can learn about an animal, the better they are at classifying it.

SPINELESS CREATURES

You have a lot more in common with a dolphin or pigeon than a mosquito or crab. These other animals are invertebrates. Invertebrates are animals that do not have backbones. There are many different types of spineless creatures, including insects, spiders, crabs, and worms. There are many, many more types of invertebrates than vertebrates. In fact, over 95% of all animals on Earth are invertebrates with insects being the most numerous. There are literally millions of different species of insects crawling, slithering, and flying around.

CASE STUDY:
Beetles!

Beetles are the invertebrate kings of the planet. If aliens wrote a guidebook about what lives on Earth, you could bet they'd talk about beetles. There are about 400,000 different types of beetles on the planet, the largest animal group by far! Compare this to only about 50,000 total types of vertebrates. In fact, there are more types of beetles than all the mammals, birds, reptiles, and fish combined.

MEET SOME INVERTEBRATES

Insects

Worms

Shellfish

Invertebrates were the first animals to evolve from single-cell organisms and have no bones or skeletons, although some have developed exoskeletons—a hard outer covering, such as shell, that protects them. Invertebrates are much smaller than vertebrates and have less complex brains, but they are well-suited for survival.

VASCULAR AND NONVASCULAR PLANTS

You now know that animals can be divided into two different categories: those with backbones and those without backbones. Like animals, plants also have a classification system.

MOVING WATER AND FOOD

All cells need water, and plants are divided into two groups based on how they deliver water to their cells. These two types are **vascular plants** and **nonvascular plants**. Vascular plants have an organized system to move water and food to their cells. They use roots to absorb water and a tissue called xylem (*zy-lum*) to move it upward to the shoots. Another plant part called phloem (*floe-em*) moves sugars and other helpful molecules to the plant's cells. Think of xylem and phloem as a vast highway system, trucking important chemicals throughout the plant. Most land plants are vascular plants, including trees, flowers, shrubs, and the plants that produce fruit and vegetables.

A slice of a buttercup stem magnified 1,000 times. Can you see all the tiny straw-like chambers?

CASE STUDY:
Vascular Vegetables

Celery is a great plant for observing a vascular system in action. *Materials: a stalk of fresh celery • a glass of water • red food coloring • plastic knife • stir stick.*

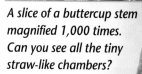

1. *Carefully cut the white end off the celery. You should be able to see the vascular bundles of xylem and phloem in the celery.*
2. *Add 2 drops of food coloring to the water. Stir.*
3. *Put the end of the celery in the glass of water. Wait a few hours (or even overnight).*
4. *Take the celery out of the water. What do you observe? The celery should be streaked with color because the vascular system of the plant lets water move easily through it. Cut the celery apart where the streaks are, to see even more details. Vascular plants are terrific water-movers.*

THE TALLEST OF THE TALL
Redwoods are the tallest trees on Earth, and they can grow as high as a 30-story building thanks to their vascular system.

Moss

Liverwort

Hornwort

ANCIENT PLANTS

Some plants do not have a "superhighway" to transport water and nutrients. These kinds of plants are called nonvascular plants. These feathery, spongy plants are some of the most ancient types of plants and first sprouted about 460 million years ago.

Examples of nonvascular plants are mosses, liverworts, and hornworts. Because they cannot easily move water, nonvascular plants need to live in damp areas and grow low to the ground, usually no more than a few centimeters. They don't have true roots, stems, or leaves. Instead of producing seeds like their vascular cousins, nonvascular plants use spores to reproduce.

ANCIENT PLANTS

Mosses, liverworts, and hornworts are some of the oldest plants around. Scientists believe these plants began as shallow water dwellers. They are relatives of algae —the greenish slime that forms on ponds.

WHY SORT?

Think about the number of different species in the world: Over 300,000 different types of plants, about 50,000 different vertebrates, and a staggering 1,300,000 (and still counting) invertebrates. Classification systems help organize organisms in order to better understand their similarities and differences.

WHAT'S MY ORGANISM?

Think of an organism and then use this classification key to determine which group it belongs to.

Does it produce its own food?

YES → **It's a plant.**

NO → **It's an animal.**

Does it have an organized system to transport water and food?

Does it have a backbone?

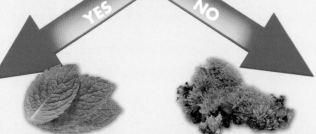

It's a vascular plant.

It's a nonvascular plant.

It's a vertebrate.

It's an invertebrate.

103

HOW ORGANISMS SURVIVE

Food, water, protection from harm—every organism needs these things to live.

You think you've got it tough? Try being a ruby-throated hummingbird. You'd have to collect and eat *more* than your own weight each day. You would have to fly hundreds of miles through heavy winds and storms to escape bone-chilling cold as you follow the warm weather that will bring you food. And don't forget there are plenty of other animals who would just love to turn you into a bite-sized snack. Surviving is hard work!

In order to survive, all organisms need these things: water, an energy source (food), and protection from harsh weather and other organisms.

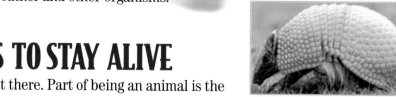

Where's the hare?

WAYS TO STAY ALIVE

It's a tough world out there. Part of being an animal is the fact that some other animal is hoping to turn you into its lunch. To survive, animals have evolved many different ways to defend themselves against predators. Some animals **camouflage** themselves so they can't easily be spotted. For example, the snowshoe hare grows brown fur during the summer and white fur during winter to blend in with its surroundings.

Would you eat a sandwich that smelled terrible? Probably not. Animals such as skunks and some insects make stinky smells that repulse would-be attackers. Turtles, rhinos, and sea urchins grow their own natural armor for protection.

A sea urchin

Another adaptation is called **mimicry**, when one animal behaves, sounds, smells, or looks like another animal. For example, the false cobra is a fairly harmless snake that looks so much like the poisonous cobra that other animals tend to leave it alone. Finally, animals can use speed and their own senses (such as keen hearing and smell) to avoid getting caught.

HAVING A BALL
Some armadillos roll up into tight armor-plated balls to protect themselves.

TWO ANIMALS, TWO STRATEGIES

Getting food and water isn't always easy. The Namibian web-footed gecko (below) lives in a dry desert. It gets water by letting early-morning mist collect on its eyeballs, and then licking it off!

Leaf-cutter ants are considered the first farmers. These insects cut down leaves, put them in a "garden," and then their ant babies eat the fungus that grows on the leaves!

TIME TO DINE

All animals must eat to survive, and they have many different ways to get their food. Carnivores (animals that eat other animals) tend to be stealthy, patient hunters. Some carnivores such as polar bears, wolves, and owls rely on powerful muscles and sharp teeth or claws to catch their prey. Orcas, hyenas, and lions use teamwork when hunting for food, increasing their chances for a decent meal.

Many animals are omnivores (eating both animals and plants) or herbivores (eating only plants). And speaking of plants—why don't we eat hay? Cows, koalas, and horses can digest hay because of unicellular organisms that live in their stomachs. These tiny organisms *also* must eat to survive, so they digest hay. We humans do not have these tiny bacteria in our stomachs so hay is inedible to us.

Some animals have a special behavioral adaptation for surviving during times with little food. Most bears find it difficult to find enough fish, nuts, and berries in the winter, so they **hibernate** during the coldest months when their food supplies are low. Other animals, such as chipmunks, squirrels, skunks, and bats are cold-weather snoozers too.

PLANT POWER

Plants have a different set of adaptations that allow them to survive. Some produce poisons to prevent them from becoming a meal for a hungry animal. Others grow thorns or thick bark to shield them from attack. All plants need water. Some plants—called deciduous (*dih-sid-you-us*) plants—become **dormant**, shedding their leaves in winter to conserve water and save energy. Plants also compete for sunlight. Trees are the masters of growing tall to capture more sunlight than the smaller plants beneath them.

All plants also need nutrients, which they normally absorb through the soil. Some plants, such as the Venus flytrap and the pitcher plant, grow in places with nutrient poor soil, so they have evolved the ability to digest insects to get the nutrients they need. These plants still make their own food by harvesting the element carbon from the air through photosynthesis. Think of the insects that they "eat" as being a bit like vitamins for the plant.

An ouch waiting to happen! Sharp thorns keep predators away.

SURVIVOR!

Think about all the things you do every day to survive. Imagine what your life would be like without shelter, food, or clean water.

CASE STUDY: Failure to Survive

If all members of a particular species fail to survive, it is called extinction.

Some scientists estimate that 99% of all species that ever lived are now extinct, almost all by natural causes. Unfortunately, human pollution and habitat destruction have recently caused many species to become extinct and many more species are now threatened.

One example is the Chinese river dolphin. It has not been seen since 2002 and is now believed to be extinct.

Overfishing, pollution, and human development share the blame.

A photo of one of the last Chinese river dolphins.

RECAP AND REVIEW

PLANT CELL

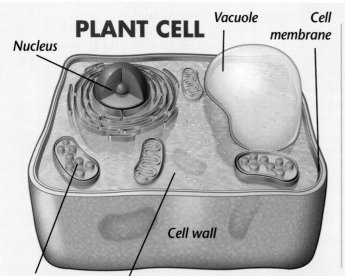

Nucleus

Vacuole

Cell membrane

Cell wall

Chloroplast Cytoplasm

ANIMAL CELL

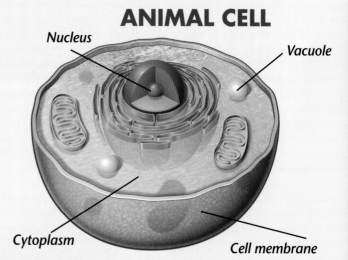

Nucleus

Vacuole

Cytoplasm

Cell membrane

Plants

ORGANISMS CAN BE GROUPED INTO CATEGORIES

Animals

Vascular
Has special tissues to transport food and water

Nonvascular
Does NOT have special tissues to transport food and water

Vertebrate
Has a backbone

Invertebrate
Does NOT have a backbone

Trees

Flowering plants

Ferns

Moss

Liverwort

Hornwort

Mammals

Reptiles

Birds

Jellyfish

Mollusks

Insects

Use pages 90-91 to answer question 1.

1. What are cells?

Use pages 92-93 to answer question 2.

2. There are four different types of specialized cells listed on page 92. What are those cells and how are they different from one another?

Use pages 94-95 to answer questions 3 and 4.

3. Draw and label the parts of a plant cell and the parts of an animal cell.

4. Describe the role of each labeled part of an animal and plant cell.

Use pages 96-97 to answer questions 5 and 6.

5. How are scientists able to observe and analyze cells?

6. Think about the differences between plants and animals. Why do you think plant cells need cell walls and animal cells do not?

Use pages 98-99 to answer question 7.

7. What is the difference between a unicellular organism and a multicellular organism?

Use pages 100-101 to answer question 8.

8. How can animals be grouped? What is the difference between the groups? What are some examples in each group?

Use pages 102-103 to answer question 9.

9. How can plants be grouped? What is the difference between the groups? What are some examples in each group?

Use pages 104-105 to answer questions 10 and 11.

10. What do organisms need to have in order to survive?

11. Organisms use specific adaptations to help them survive in their environment. Identify and explain three of these adaptations.

DATA DETETCTIVE

The following list contains some endangered vertebrate species living in the world today. Copy and complete the chart by classifying each species.

- **Blue Whale**
- **Fiji Crested Iguana**
- **Aruba Island Rattlesnake**
- **Tiger**
- **European Eel**
- **Gorilla**
- **Steller Sea Lion**
- **Red-crowned Crane**
- **Parrot**
- **Chinese Alligator**
- **Bactrian Camel**
- **Chinese Giant Salamander**
- **Atlantic Salmon**
- **Bald Eagle**

FISH	MAMMAL	BIRD	AMPHIBIAN	REPTILE

YOU ARE THE SCIENTIST

Studying a jellyfish or armadillo can help us better understand the world. Why do scientists want to learn about the specific traits of organisms that allow those organisms to survive in their environment? How can knowledge about other species be helpful to humans?

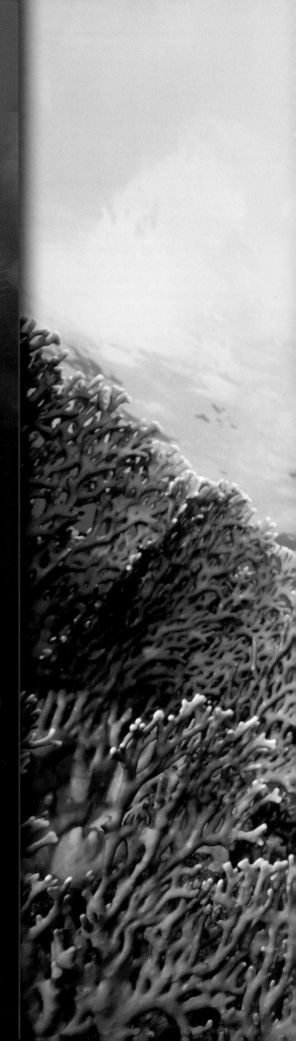

CHAPTER SIX

A plankton (shown greatly enlarged)

THE OCEANS

Deep beneath the ocean waves there is a strange and beautiful realm. It is a place of danger, mystery, and startling contrasts. It is home to the world's largest living creatures and the world's longest mountain range. If you were to dive to its deepest spot, the pressure would crush you, yet dozens of species manage to live and thrive many miles down.

Come explore a world that few have ever seen.

A hawksbill sea turtle swims close to a coral. Corals may look like underwater plants, but they are actually invertebrate animals. They are made of millions of teeny predators that have clustered together into colonies.

Have you ever been to the ocean? Maybe you played in the waves or picked up shells, but there is so much more happening under the water. Without our oceans, Earth would simply be a hot, lifeless rock.

THE WORLD BENEATH THE WAVES

Maybe Earth isn't the best name for our planet. After all, there is a lot more ocean than land! More than 70% of Earth's surface is covered with vast stretches of cool, shimmering, rolling, crashing, salty, blue-green liquid. The existence of the oceans is what sets us apart from all our fellow planets and it is the source of all life.

SEVENTY PERCENT OF OUR PLANET

Ocean waters can go from smooth and calm to dangerous and deadly in a matter of moments, but the seas are still a great mystery to us. Almost ninety percent of our planet's life forms live in the sea. Fearsome creatures unleash powerful poisons that can kill instantly. Gelatin-like blobs light up like carnival glow sticks. Creatures as long as a basketball court survive on a diet of tiny morsels, each only 5 cm long. Strange worms survive by "eating" chemicals instead of food. And of course, there are all sorts of beautiful fish in rainbows of bright colors and patterns.

A shrimp

An eel

A sea-horse

OCEAN? SEA? WHAT'S THE DIFFERENCE?

People often use "ocean" and "sea" to describe the same thing. When talking about specific physical geography, the two terms have slightly different meanings. A sea is smaller than an ocean and is more enclosed by land, but to some species, such as whales, there are no boundaries between the two bodies of water.

Microplankton

Magnified 400 times

GRAB YOUR SCUBA GEAR

Let's explore the oceans in three different ways.

1. Geological characteristics: What does it look like more than ten kilometers beneath the waves? Are there really mountain ranges and volcanoes down there?

2. Physical characteristics: How do waves form? What causes the tides and ocean currents? What is so vitally important about the saltiness of seawater?

3. Ecological characteristics: Meet some of the fascinating creatures and plants that call the ocean "home." Now let's dive in!

A lionfish

SCIENTISTS IN THE SPOTLIGHT: DIVING IN THE DEEP

Exploring the deepest parts of the ocean floor presents many challenges. The deeper you dive, the greater the pressure of all the water above you. At the very deepest part of the ocean—over 11 km below the surface—the weight is crushing. It is like having 50 jumbo jets stacked on top of you, so designing a vehicle that can withstand that pressure is a real feat.

A famous Hollywood film producer joined with deep-sea engineers to build a new type of submersible and, in 2012, plummeted to the deepest part of the ocean, the Mariana Trench. This vehicle will give scientists a better view and easier access to the mysterious life forms in the ocean's deepest reaches. Samples of sea bottom along with its microorganisms are now being studied and will soon provide new data about life at the very bottom of the ocean.

James Cameron's submersible heads to the deepest part of the ocean.

The Earth did not always have oceans. At one time it is was a lifeless ball of poisonous air and scalding rock.

HOW THE OCEANS FORMED

If you could travel back in time to the Earth of four billion years ago, you would see nothing but molten, jagged rocks. There was no liquid water anywhere. The heat was blistering. So what happened? How did Earth go from being a planet with no visible water to a planet where oceans cover more than seventy percent of the globe?

A FIERY HOT ROCK

This is what Earth may have looked like 3.8 billion years ago. Imagine nothing but fiery rocks and the constant pelting of asteroids.

These five paintings, based on scientific findings, show how the Earth might have looked as the oceans formed.

Asteroids smashed into a red-hot Earth.

GREAT CHANGES

Our current scientific understanding is that the solar system began as a huge, whirling cloud of dust and gases. Over time, gravity pulled these materials together to form our sun, the planets, asteroids (orbiting chunks of rock), and comets (orbiting chunks of ice and dust).

When the Earth was about one billion years old, things began to change. The very hot rocks of the Earth were releasing gases that spewed from thousands and thousands of volcanoes. At the same time, comets and meteorites, also carrying gases, constantly bombarded the Earth, which at that time did not have a protective atmosphere.

You might recognize the names of some of these gases: methane and ammonia, mixed with water vapor and carbon dioxide. These formed a cloud of toxic gas that swirled around and around until the air was so thick it blocked some of the sun's rays and the temperatures began to drop. About 3.8 billion years ago the temperature finally dipped below 100°C and the gases began to cool. Cooling gases led to condensation and all that condensation brought rain. Lots and lots and <u>lots</u> of rain. Hundreds and hundreds of years of rain. The endless rain began to collect in low-lying areas and the first oceans began to form.

Trapped gases from deep within the Earth burst forth. These gases rose up into the atmosphere.

FROM HOT AND DRY TO COOL AND WET

By three billion years ago, the Earth was vastly changed from its hot and rocky origins. The waters of the new oceans were greatly affected by the pull of the moon, which was then much closer than it is today. Enormous tides tugged at the waters, constantly churning them as the moon made its daily pull on the oceans.

The rising gases condensed into clouds, which brought many hundreds of years of torrential rain. This constant rain began to fill the Earth's craters.

METEORS IN VIRGINIA

In the years after World War II, the population of Virginia began to grow. Would there be enough drinking water? In 1983, the search for additional aquifers near the Chesapeake Bay led to an an astonishing discovery. Test drillings revealed rock samples that <u>had</u> to have come from a meteor! After carefully analyzing the rock samples, scientists were able to conclude that the Chesapeake Bay had been shaped by a meteor strike over 35 million years ago that left a crater more than 90 km in diameter!

Chesapeake Bay
N
15 miles
Windmill Point
Mathews County
Cape Charles
Crater outline
Newport News Park
Kiptopeke
Moores Bridges
NASA Langley Research Center
Virginia Beach
ATLANTIC OCEAN

LIFE BEGINS

Perhaps the most amazing event is this: About three and a half billion years ago, the first life forms began to stir in the seas. These single-celled, microscopic organisms were the start of all the diverse organisms that inhabit our planet today. Scientists can trace the beginnings of life to those warm, salty ocean waters when the first single-celled microbes formed.

Mists covered much of the Earth, as rainfall spilled over the crater edges and merged into one vast body of water. Volcanoes continued to spew gas and moisture into the air.

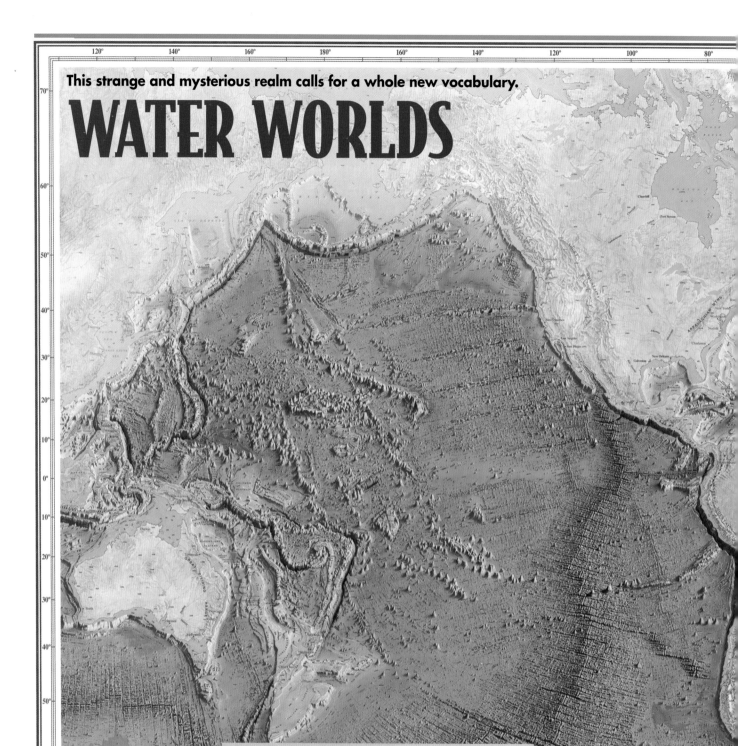

This strange and mysterious realm calls for a whole new vocabulary.

WATER WORLDS

KEY WORDS TO KNOW

CONTINENTAL SHELF
The underwater edge of a continent.

CONTINENTAL SLOPE
A steep slope that separates the continental shelf from the deep ocean basin.

CONTINENTAL RISE
The area at the bottom of the continental slope. It is a vast underwater hill made from tons of accumulated sediment.

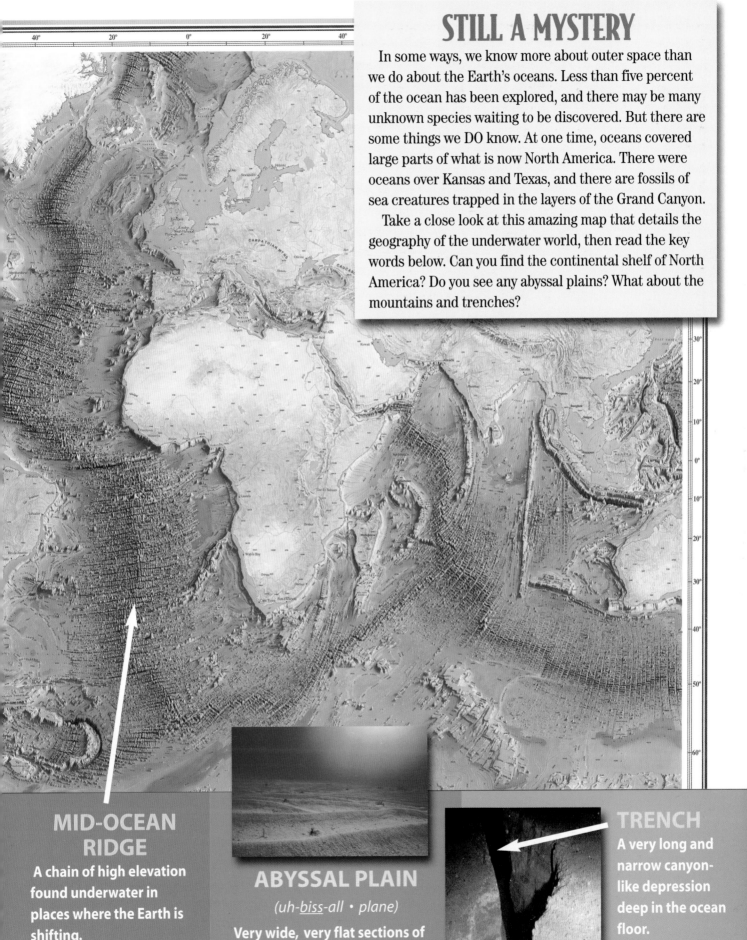

STILL A MYSTERY

In some ways, we know more about outer space than we do about the Earth's oceans. Less than five percent of the ocean has been explored, and there may be many unknown species waiting to be discovered. But there are some things we DO know. At one time, oceans covered large parts of what is now North America. There were oceans over Kansas and Texas, and there are fossils of sea creatures trapped in the layers of the Grand Canyon.

Take a close look at this amazing map that details the geography of the underwater world, then read the key words below. Can you find the continental shelf of North America? Do you see any abyssal plains? What about the mountains and trenches?

MID-OCEAN RIDGE
A chain of high elevation found underwater in places where the Earth is shifting.

ABYSSAL PLAIN
(uh-_biss_-all • _plane_)

Very wide, very flat sections of the deep ocean floor, made of thick layers of sediment.

TRENCH
A very long and narrow canyon-like depression deep in the ocean floor.

There is a lot more to the bottom of the sea than just sand.

THE OCEAN FLOOR

The oceans may look flat from here on dry land, but underneath they are anything but! There are several important parts to the ocean bottom.

WADING INTO THE OCEAN

When you go to the beach and walk out into the water, you are standing on the beginning of the **continental shelf**. It is the part that extends from Earth's land masses. Think of it as the underwater portion of a continent. Picture the land close to the seashore—the hills, small ridges, and valleys. The continental shelf looks very much like that. It just happens to be under the water. In some places the shelf extends out for hundreds of miles. In others it barely exists. The "deep sea" begins at the place where the continental shelf suddenly steeply dives deeper.

The continental shelf along the Atlantic coast.

A STEEP SLOPE

This enormous drop happens at a place called the **continental slope**. It is here, where the water is about 200 meters deep, that the shelf ends. Swoop down to the bottom of the continental slope, and you are suddenly between 2,000 and 3,000 meters below the surface—about a mile and a half down.

The place where the slope ends is called the **continental rise**. The rise is an underwater area made from millions of tons of accumulated sediment—all the debris that drifts down from above, such as dead fish, decaying plants, animal wastes, and soil and rock that have washed into the water from the shore. All this material settles on the continental rise in a thick layer.

200 m	Continental Shelf
	Continental Slope
2,000-3,000 m	Continental Rise
4,000-6,000 m	Abyssal Plain
10,000 m	Ocean Trench

Underwater volcanoes form in hot spots in the Earth's mantle. Hawaii has one of the most famous ones.

UNDER THE SEA
An artist imagines what the ocean floor might look like if you could slice through it.

Continental Shelf

Continental Slope

Continental Rise

Ocean Trench

Abyssal Plain

A VAST PLAIN

The continental rise gives way to the next segment of ocean floor—the **abyssal plain**.

Flat, flatter, flattest—that's the abyssal plain

Much like the vast Great Plains areas of North America, the abyssal plains cover much of the ocean bottom. The abyssal plains are usually found at depths between 4,000 and 6,000 meters. They are among the flattest, smoothest, and least explored regions on Earth, yet there are still even deeper parts of the ocean.

DEEPEST OF THE DEEP

The ocean's deep **trenches** are long, narrow valleys formed by movements of the Earth's solid outer layer. The deepest part of the ocean is at a place known as the Mariana Trench—a huge chasm that is 2,500 km long and over 70 km wide. In that trench, about 320 km southwest of Guam, you will find the absolute deepest point on Earth. It is known as "Challenger Deep," and it is a staggering 11 km below sea level.

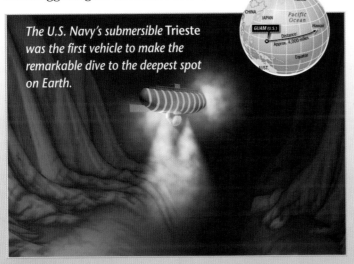

The U.S. Navy's submersible Trieste was the first vehicle to make the remarkable dive to the deepest spot on Earth.

HOW HIGH? HOW DEEP?

Comparing Heights and Depths

Jet cruises at 10,688 m

Mt. Everest 8,848 m

Mauna Kea*

The Mariana Trench 11,033 m

Mt. Rainier, WA 4,392 m

Mt. Rogers, VA 1,746 m

* Total height: 10,200 m
4,200 m above sea level
6,000 m below sea level

Parts of the ocean floor look like the surface of Earth, but on an even grander scale. Along with the vast abyssal plains, there are also towering peaks. The world's longest (65,000 km) and highest mountain range—is underwater.

This enormous mountain range is in an area where layers of the Earth's crust keep spreading apart. All this activity makes it a very volatile place with many volcanoes and earthquakes. Why? As the crust spreads apart a new seafloor is created, but until it hardens it is like a door to the hot molten core of the Earth and powerful hydrothermal vents and volcanoes emerge.

There are other strange things happening beneath the waves—such as these deep sea "smokers."

UNDERWATER CHIMNEYS!

Hydrothermal vents, called smokers, form at mid-ocean ridges. As scalding magma (molten rock) comes into contact with icy seawater, it hardens to form chimneys of rock. Some of these are 40 meters high. Some amazing organisms call these vents home-sweet-home, surviving on the chemicals that spew out.

Mid-Ocean Ridge

Abyssal Plain

You now know what it looks like under the water, but what is happening <u>in</u> it?

THE OCEAN IN MOTION

Winds blow. Tides rise and fall. Gravity tugs. The sun shines. As a result, Earth's waters are constantly kept in motion. One of those motions is called a **current**. Huge amounts of water are pushed great distances, swirling around all the continents as they go. Throw a message in a bottle off the waters of Virginia Beach and it just might eventually end up in England.

DUCKS ON THE MOVE

On a storm-tossed January night in 1992, a shipping crate filled with 29,000 plastic bath toys was flung overboard in the middle of the Pacific Ocean. And so began a strange and amazing journey that reveals many of the mysteries of the Earth's ocean currents.

What happened to the rubber ducks? Scientists have been tracking the journeys of the plastic toys for many years now, with surprising results. 19,000 bobbed south and washed up on beaches in Australia and South America. The rest floated north, up to the Arctic Ocean, then down along the coast of North America where a very powerful current pushed them across the Atlantic Ocean and on toward Europe—an astounding 27,000 kilometer journey!

THE GULF STREAM

There are seven major global currents, but the one that impacts us here in Virginia is called the **Gulf Stream**. The Gulf Stream is part of a large current system that starts off the shores of Mexico, then flows north through the Gulf of Mexico and swings around Florida's east coast. When it reaches North Carolina, it begins to drift off into the North Atlantic, traveling at a speed of over nine kilometers an hour on its surface. It carries huge volumes of warm water across the Atlantic, which keeps many parts of Western Europe much warmer than countries at the same latitudes in North America or Asia.

DANGER

STRONG CURRENT

The Gulf Stream

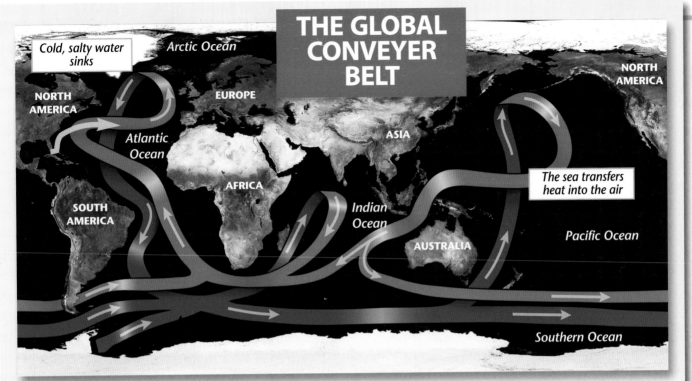

THE GLOBAL CONVEYER BELT

Cold, salty water sinks

Arctic Ocean

NORTH AMERICA

EUROPE

NORTH AMERICA

ASIA

Atlantic Ocean

AFRICA

The sea transfers heat into the air

SOUTH AMERICA

Indian Ocean

Pacific Ocean

AUSTRALIA

Southern Ocean

WARM SHALLOW CURRENT

DEEP COLD CURRENT

GULF STREAM

How does a current keep moving? Think of an escalator. It carries you to the next floor, but then it loops back down where you cannot see it to return back to the floor below. Ocean currents do the same thing. They carry warm surface waters from tropical areas toward the polar regions. There, the waters cool and the colder, denser waters sink and flow south in the deep ocean keeping the waters moving.

A satellite image shows the movement of the currents.

HOT AND COLD RUNNING WATER

The map below was made by a satellite that has special infrared sensors that "see" heat to monitor the oceans' temperatures. You can see the Gulf Stream in red flowing along the east coast of the United States (in black).

The orange and red show the warmest temperatures (22-25°C) while purple and blue indicate the coldest temperatures (5-15°C).

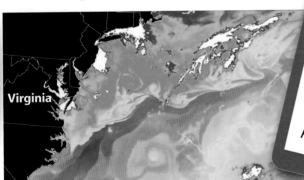

Virginia

CASE STUDY:
When Warm Meets Cold

You'll need 2 clear plastic cups, a pitcher of ice water, pepper, a cup of hot tap water, and food coloring.

1. Fill one clear plastic cup two-thirds full with ice water. Sprinkle some pepper on the surface of the water and let it settle.

2. Add several drops of food coloring to the hot water. Slowly pour some of the hot water into the ice water. What happened?

3. Observe as the hot water cools. What happens? What happened to the pepper?

4. Repeat the experiment, but this time start with a cup of very hot tap water. Pour colored ice water into the cup. What do you predict will happen? Why? How does this relate to currents?

Stand at the seashore and stick out your tongue. You can taste the saltiness in the air. But why is the ocean salty?

SALINITY

Where did all the salt in the seas come from? Surprise! Most of it comes from the land. Many rocks have compounds of sodium and chlorine in them. In fact, you probably have sprinkled ground-up bits of these dietary minerals on your french fries. They are in every saltshaker in America!

SALT OF THE EARTH

Millions of years of rain, combined with water flowing down from the mountains into rivers and streams, have washed a lot of the salt out of the Earth's rocks. As rivers flow into the ocean, they carry salt. So why are rivers freshwater and not salt water?

As the sun shines down on the broad expanses of the ocean, the waters keep evaporating. Salt does not evaporate so the water keeps getting saltier. Rivers only carry small amounts of salt, but there are many, *many* rivers dumping water into the oceans so the salt just keeps coming, like thousands of faucets filling a giant bathtub. Some ocean salt also comes from hydrothermal vents and underwater volcanoes. We call the level of salt in the water **salinity**.

SALT AND CURRENTS

Salt plays a really important role in the movement of ocean currents. Salty water is heavier than fresh water. As the saltier water cools, it sinks downward, layering underneath the warmer, less salty water. This icy cold, salty water has a greater **density** than warmer, less salty water. That means it has more mass. Imagine tossing a beach ball and a bowling ball into the ocean. What would happen? The bowling ball will sink, while the beach ball will float. Icy salt water does something similar to that heavy bowling ball. The combination of heavier, saltier water below and lighter, warmer, less salty water above creates a slow, steady stirring of the Earth's seas.

SHOVELING SALT
A worker collects salt from evaporated seawater that was left out in the sun in shallow seaside pools.

THE DEEP BLUE SEA

Salt, sunshine, and the **depth** of the oceans are what powers the "global conveyor belt." This slow, steady stirring of the Earth's oceans is vitally important to the food chain. Deep waters are very rich in nutrients. As the currents push the waters, the nutrient-rich deep waters keep mixing with nutrient-depleted surface waters. This helps algae and seaweed to grow, which in turn supports many other forms of life.

There are about 2,000 grains of salt in a tablespoon of seawater. Scientists measure the salinity of the Earth's waters by "parts per thousand," calculating how many grams of salt there are in 1,000 milliliters (1 liter) of water. Most oceans average about 35 on this scale, but the Dead Sea, a body of water in the Middle East, gets almost a 300! It is so salty that no fish can live in it, but all the extra salt makes it easy to float in. Perfect for reading a book while swimming!

CASE STUDY:
The Effects of Salinity

You'll need a large glass partially filled with very warm tap water, a raw egg, a small apple, a small pebble, a cup of salt, and a measuring spoon

1. *Place the egg in the water-filled glass. It should sink to the bottom.*

2. *Now add 1 teaspoon of salt to the glass and gently stir it. Keep adding teaspoons of salt until the egg begins to float to the surface. Record how many teaspoons you had to add.*

3. *Can you infer why this happens? How does this affect people who swim in salt water? Now repeat the experiment using the pebble and apple in place of the egg. How many teaspoons of salt did you need to get each item to float? Explain your results. What conclusions can be made?*

SURVIVING AT SEA
People have managed to survive for weeks at sea with no drinking water. How? They gathered rainwater and early morning condensation in scraps of their clothing. Can you imagine having only dewdrops to drink?

DON'T DRINK THE SEAWATER!

Imagine you have been shipwrecked. You are floating around in the ocean in a small lifeboat and you are getting <u>very</u> thirsty. All that water is looking very tempting! What would happen if you drank a few glasses of seawater? Surely just a few glasses could not hurt?

Surprisingly, our bodies actually have a lot in common with seawater. Grown-ups have enough salt in their bodies to fill almost three saltshakers. If you have ever tasted your tears, you can taste the salt. Sweating, crying, and urinating all help rid the body of extra salt. But too much salt in your body brings disaster.

When the body has too much salt, water molecules from every cell rush out to try to help dilute the excess salt. Now your cells don't have enough water to do their jobs—such as pumping blood or nourishing your brain. An accidental gulp or two of seawater won't hurt you, but remember—don't ever drink a lot of seawater!

WAVES AND TIDES

Waves most commonly occur because of another "w" word—wind. When winds blow across the water's surface, they create friction. The friction between water and wind creates a ripple. Hold your palm out flat in front of your mouth and blow out a little puff. Now blow again—a little longer this time. Now blow out with all your might. That same action, carried out by the wind, will determine if a ripple will grow into a wave.

CATCHING A "WAVE"

Why do oceans have big waves, but lakes and bays do not? It has to do with the length of the open water over which the wind can blow. Pretend a soup bowl is a lake. The wind can only blow from rim to rim. At a real lake, the wind can blow from one shore to the other. That's pretty far, but not as far as across an ocean! In oceans, since the wind can blow over huge distances, much bigger waves can build up than in lakes and bays.

Here's a surprising fact. In deep water, a wave is actually energy moving forward, not water. The water molecules in the waves move in a circular motion and return to their starting point with each roll. The water in a wave does not move forward, but the energy does.

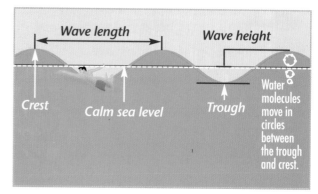

Wave length • Wave height • Crest • Calm sea level • Trough • Water molecules move in circles between the trough and crest.

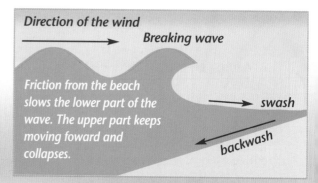

Direction of the wind • Breaking wave • Friction from the beach slows the lower part of the wave. The upper part keeps moving foward and collapses. • swash • backwash

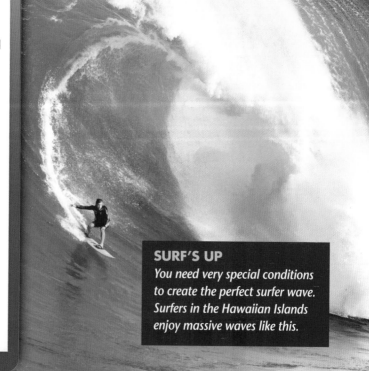

CASE STUDY:
Making Waves

There are three main factors in how waves form. Fill a rectangular pan with water, get your mouth even with one end, and b-l-o-w! Record what happened.

1. Speed of the wind
A little or a lot: The faster the wind is blowing, the bigger the wave will be. Experiment with blowing out a gentle little puff; then blow harder.

2. The duration of the wind
Short or long: Waves get larger when longer gusts hit them. Try a short, quick blow, and then a longer blow.

3. The distance the wind blows
Near or far: The maximum length of open water over which the wind can blow will affect wave size. Blow all the way across the pan and notice what happens. Then put your mouth at the middle of the pan and start blowing from there. Are the waves different sizes now?

SURF'S UP
You need very special conditions to create the perfect surfer wave. Surfers in the Hawaiian Islands enjoy massive waves like this.

TIDES AND THE OCEANS

Wind plays a huge part on the movement of the oceans but it has company—tides. Tides are the result of gravity—the powerful attraction between the sun, moon, and Earth. Because it is so much closer to Earth, the moon has a more powerful impact on tides than does the sun. The gravity of the moon is always tugging at the Earth, just as Earth's gravity pulls on the moon. This force is not strong enough to pull you and rocks away from Earth, but it is strong enough to pull on liquid water.

If you have ever tried to hold water in your hands, you know how hard it is to do. Water is fluid and it is always moving. When a place on Earth, such as Virginia, is feeling the pull of the moon's gravity, it will have a high tide. As the Earth rotates, and we spin away, we feel less of the moon's gravity, so the tides get lower.

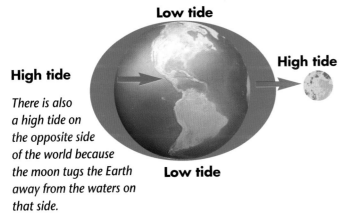

In some places the tides are so extreme that boats are left sitting in the mud until the tide rises once again.

Low tide

High tide

High tide

There is also a high tide on the opposite side of the world because the moon tugs the Earth away from the waters on that side.

Low tide

STIR IT UP

All this constant moving of the waters has a big effect on ocean currents. As the tides rise and fall, currents speed up midway through each cycle. All this movement has a beneficial side. Rising and falling tides keep ice from forming in harbors in colder climates, and some countries are learning how to use the daily rise and fall of tides to generate electricity. After all, the tides are more predictable than wind energy or solar power.

KILLER WAVES

At 2:46 p.m., on a cold, gray day in March of 2011, the Earth's tectonic plates suddenly shifted deep beneath the ocean about 72 km off the coast of northern Japan. That shift led to the fifth most powerful earthquake ever recorded.

For six endless minutes everything shook violently. Then it grew quiet. Sirens wailed throughout Japan's coastal towns and cities warning that a **tsunami**—*a huge surge of water—would soon be arriving. It was urgent to move inland away from the coast as quickly as possible. Still, most people stayed calm. The government had built high concrete barriers to protect Japan from tsunamis, but they soon discovered the walls weren't tall enough. It only took 30 minutes for the first giant wave of water to wash in. Several more waves followed. Within a few minutes, whole towns were destroyed by the enormous, crushing weight of the walls of water.*

Tsunamis waves in the deep ocean can reach speeds of 800 km an hour.

Tsunamis are sometimes called tidal waves, but they are not the same thing. Tsunamis are caused by undersea earthquakes that violently push the water upward. This energy then moves out in all directions, eventually reaching land as a large wall of water.

Tidal waves are different. Tidal waves are caused by the effects of gravity on the water. When the gravitational pull is particularly strong because of where the moon and sun are in relation to the Earth, the tide surges in very quickly and with great power. These waves can be very dangerous, but they don't create giant walls of water like tsunamis do.

123

Almost 90 percent of the Earth's life forms dwell in the oceans, but the deeper we dive, the stranger the creatures get!

LIFE BENEATH THE WAVES

Imagine that you had superpowers and could somehow dive all the way down to the very deepest part of the ocean floor—over eleven crushing kilometers below the surface. Along the way you would pass through several layers, each with its own unique life forms.

A giant jellyfish

BOTTOMS UP!

Most of the undersea dwellers live in the sunlight zone, a band that teems with life. Here the warming rays of the sun provide the perfect atmosphere for underwater plants, algae, and phytoplankton to grow in abundance. These organisms form the basis for the undersea food web.

As the depth of the water increases, the temperature drops, the pressure increases, and the amount of light decreases. These factors influence the life forms at each depth. Creatures like the giant squid that live in the twilight and midnight zones often zip up to the sunlight zone at night to feast on the yummy edibles that live there. Deeper down in the midnight zone it is pitch black. The sea life here must provide their own light, so these creatures glow in the dark or make their own internal electricity.

An Indonesian flying fish

The animals in the lowest levels can go for long periods without eating. They survive on tiny bits of dead plant materials and animal waste that "snow" down from above. Sometimes, a whole dead whale will drift toward the bottom and they can truly feast. They also have bodies that can withstand the tremendous water pressure.

EXTREME LIFE

Marine biologists are very excited about the creatures who live in these "extreme" environments, so the deepest parts of the ocean are a thrilling place for them to do research. We once thought all organisms on Earth depended on energy from the sun, but now know that some of the creatures at the ocean bottom have never seen the sun. They survive on a diet of chemicals made by bacteria that live within their guts. The discovery of these amazing organisms showed us that other kinds of life are possible.

One species of tubeworm

THE TIDAL ZONE

Organisms living here such as mussels, crabs, and clams must survive low tides that can leave them exposed to the sun, causing them to dry out. Winters that bring freezing temperatures are also a problem, along with land-dwelling predators like birds, bears, and humans.

THE SUNLIGHT ZONE

From the surface of the ocean down to 200 meters, the sun's rays and nutrients in the waters combine to make ideal conditions for many plants, algae, and fish. Coral reefs flourish here as well as giant schools of fish that feed on plankton—tiny, free-floating organisms. Most of the ocean's fish live here.

THE MIDDLE LEVELS

A Humboldt squid can grow to six feet.

An anglerfish flashes its spike-like teeth.

THE TWILIGHT ZONE

From 200 meters to 1,000 meters, the sun's light grows faint. There are twinkles of blobby bobbing light—creatures like jellyfish that can glow in the dark. There is a diversity of eerie life forms here. Many of these animals swim up to the sunlight zone to eat after dark.

THE MIDNIGHT ZONE

From 1,000 meters to 4,000 meters, the waters are pitch dark. The only light is made by the creatures that live here. The pressure is crushing yet many creatures have adaptations that enable them to survive here, such as huge eyes and lots of teeth. Sperm whales can dive this deep in search of food.

THE BOTTOM LEVELS

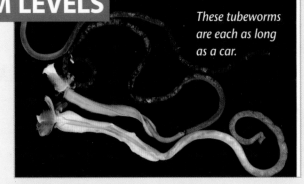

These tubeworms are each as long as a car.

THE ABYSSAL ZONE

From 4,000 meters to a depth of 6,000 meters, the water temperature hovers near zero degrees Celsius. There are very few signs of life due to the crushing pressure. But still, there are tiny squids and other sea creatures like this gorgeous sea star.

IN THE TRENCHES

What can survive in the very deepest parts of the ocean? Only a very few humans have ever been down this far to report back. There is not much life here, but what there is is amazing. Here the food chain does not depend on plants and sunlight but instead on bacteria that extract energy from chemicals.

SORTING THE SEA

The oceans teem with many different animals.

About one billion years ago, the first animal life appeared in the oceans. Today the variety of creatures that live beneath the seas is enormous. They may all look quite different, but they share two characteristics: They get their energy by eating food and they are multicellular.

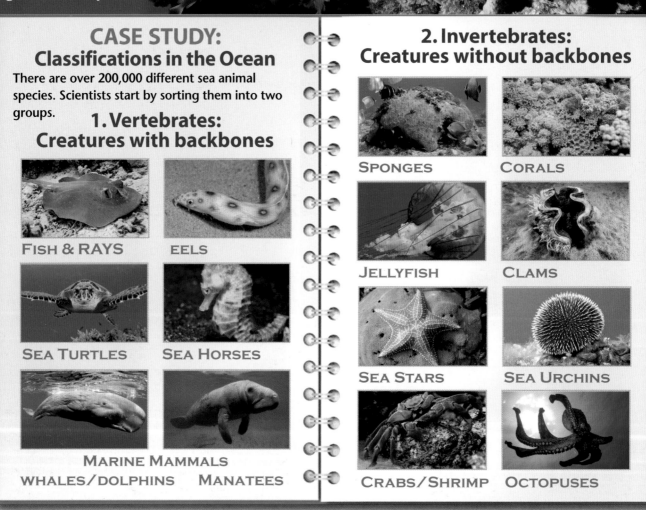

CASE STUDY:
Classifications in the Ocean

There are over 200,000 different sea animal species. Scientists start by sorting them into two groups.

1. Vertebrates:
Creatures with backbones

FISH & RAYS

EELS

SEA TURTLES

SEA HORSES

MARINE MAMMALS
WHALES/DOLPHINS   MANATEES

2. Invertebrates:
Creatures without backbones

SPONGES

CORALS

JELLYFISH

CLAMS

SEA STARS

SEA URCHINS

CRABS/SHRIMP

OCTOPUSES

SURVIVAL STRATEGIES

It would take a book of thousands of pages to describe every living deep sea creature. These are just a few of the dwellers of the deep. Each has developed unique adaptations to aid in survival. Some, like jellyfish and sea urchins, sting and stun their prey.

Others, like crabs and clams, have hard shells. You may think that fish are the most common of the ocean species, but the truth is the invertebrates outnumber the vertebrates. In fact, only about one tenth of the animals in the oceans are fish.

HIDE AND SEEK

The fish in the photo at far right have massed together to form a school that makes them appear huge to any bigger fish who dares to eat them—just one behavioral adaptation to survive in the seas. Other fish use camouflage to hide in the sand, atop rocks, or to disguise themselves as plants.

This seahorse disguises itself as seaweed.

Is it a rock or a fish?

A school of barracudas

BIGGEST OF THE BIG

Bigger than any dinosaur that ever existed, blue whales are the largest animal to have ever lived. They can grow as long as a basketball court and weigh about 200 tons when full-grown.

Whales are mammals. They do not lay eggs like fish do, but instead carry just one baby at a time, much the same way human mothers do.

Scientists believe that at one time whales were land dwellers, but about 50 million years ago, the whales started spending more time at sea. For the last 40 million years whales have been full-time ocean dwellers.

The feeding lunge of a fin whale takes about 6 seconds. See how the pouch fills with water and krill?

How do you feed a hungry whale? Blue whales are filter feeders. They have pleated pouches that expand as the whales gulp huge mouthfuls of seawater. Tiny krill get swallowed along with the water, then are trapped behind comb-like baleen—thin strands made of keratin—the same material as your fingernails. There is no escape for the krill.

Blue whales are also the loudest animals on the planet. They sing! Their sounds are loud enough to travel hundreds of miles underwater. Unlike fish, which have gills to get oxygen that is dissolved in water, whales have to breathe air. When whales come to the surface to breathe, it is easier for humans to hunt them and some species are still endangered.

A blue whale breaches the surface. Scientists cannot agree on why whales leap high out of the water.

THE THRILL OF THE KRILL
The biggest whales exist on a diet of tiny krill, each measuring about 5 cm long. It takes a lot of krill to fill a whale's belly and they eat between 4 and 8 tons a day.

DID YOU KNOW?
You can whale watch off the coast of Virginia from the end of December until the middle of March as fin whales, humpback, and right whales migrate.

127

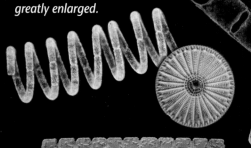
These phytoplankton are shown greatly enlarged.

We can barely see them, but these tiny specks of sea life help provide much of the Earth's oxygen.

PLANKTON

They may be teeny, but these often-microscopic, free-floating organisms play a crucial role in life, not just in the oceans but on land as well. The word **plankton** means "wanderer" in the language of ancient Greece. There are two types of plankton bobbing and drifting in the Earth's waters.

THE BLOOMING OCEANS

Phytoplankton are the most important of the ocean's creatures because they form the base of the ocean food web. These mostly plant-like organisms make their food by photosynthesis just like plants on land. Some plankton are bacteria, some are protists (single-celled non-plant organisms), but most are single-celled plants.

You will find these extraordinary organisms floating along near the top of the sunlight zone where nutrient-rich waters well up from deep below. Phytoplankton carry out most of the photosynthesis that takes place on Earth and as a result they provide much of the Earth's oxygen. Some of the most beautiful plankton are called diatoms and they are almost shell-like. They have brittle cell walls made out of silica (which is what we make glass from) and pectin which gives Jell-O its quiver.

Zooplankton are tiny animals that feed on phytoplankton and decomposing bits of dead sea life, as well as other marine animals' excretions. Many of them live lower down in the ocean's depths and travel up to the sunlight zone after dark. Some particularly delicious types of zooplankton are the larval stages of larger critters such as jellyfish, blue crabs, and many fish species when they are first born. Together, both kinds of plankton benefit not just sea dwellers but all of us land dwellers as well.

Zooplankton come in many different shapes, colors, and sizes.

"A" IS FOR ALGAE

The ancient Greeks had no microscopes with which to see the tiny sea creatures, most of which are too small to be seen with the unaided eye. But when phytoplankton mass together, they appear as a faint greenish haze due to all their chlorophyll tinting the waters.

We can actually see these miniscule organisms from space with special satellite cameras. Great swirls of phytoplankton form giant **algae** (*al*-gee) blooms in some areas of the oceans. These huge areas are a bit like the grasslands of the sea, and together with land-based plants are vital in helping to remove carbon dioxide from the atmosphere. This satellite photo shows a vast swirling mass of phytoplankton abloom in the North Atlantic near Europe.

A larval water flea, shown greatly enlarged. Larval animals are a common food for many sea dwellers.

WHAT'S THAT SLIMY STUFF?

Have you ever seen seaweed washed up onto shore? It looks a bit gross, but it is incredibly important. Up here on dry land, we use seaweed in foods such as ice cream, salad dressing, and sushi as well as in many medicines. These useful marine algae have a lot in common with land-based plants. All depend on photosynthesis, but red and brown seaweed have other pigments in addition to chlorophyll, which give them their distinctive colors.

"P" IS FOR PROCHLOROCOCCUS

(prok-lo-row-*cock*-us)
This organism may be teeny-tiny, but it is the most abundant photo-synthetic cell on the planet. A single milliliter of water can be packed with 100,000 cells or more! This one organism is thought to account for as much as half of the photosynthesis in the oceans. It is also the smallest known organism that makes its food from the sun's energy.

About one fifth of the oxygen you breathe comes from these microscopic organisms.

KELP ME!
Kelp is the largest seaweed on Earth. A healthy kelp can grow 50 cm in one day and reach a height of 50 meters. Several animal species depend on kelp for survival, such as sea urchins. The urchins, in turn, are a favorite food of otters.

Algae, seaweeds, and plankton are critical to the survival of the planet. Read on to discover why.

It's a fish-eat-fish world down there.

MARINE FOOD WEB

By now you understand what a complex world exists beneath the ocean's waves, yet virtually all the sea's creatures from the tiniest plankton to the great blue whale are linked in a food web.

FLOATING, SWIMMING, OR JUST STAYING PUT

Unlike the plants on dry land, there are two types of ocean plants. Some have roots that are attached to the ocean floor, but most are rootless phytoplankton floating along with the water.

Marine animals can be swimmers, floaters, or ocean-floor dwellers. Zooplankton are always floaters. Most marine animals are very small, but some, like jellyfish, can grow to be quite large. The zooplankton population also includes fish eggs or larval forms of organisms that will eventually grow up and become good swimmers, if they are not eaten.

Fish, octopuses, whales, rays, and eels are all great swimmers. They can move around in search of the densest, most delicious plankton patches! At the ocean floor you will find another group—critters such as lobsters, starfish, snails, and oysters. They inch their way across the ocean floor, but cannot move about much more than that.

THE OCEANS' FUTURE

For well over three billion years, the Earth's oceans and seas have nourished our planet and served as the cradle for life. Today, some of the ocean's creatures are in danger from overfishing and habitat destruction. Others have suffered due to oil spills and other "human accidents." If there is global warming, it will greatly affect the oceans and those who live near its shores. The job of saving the oceans is the key to the future of the Earth. The oceans are fragile. It is up to us to take care of them because healthy oceans are necessary for our own health, and that of our planet.

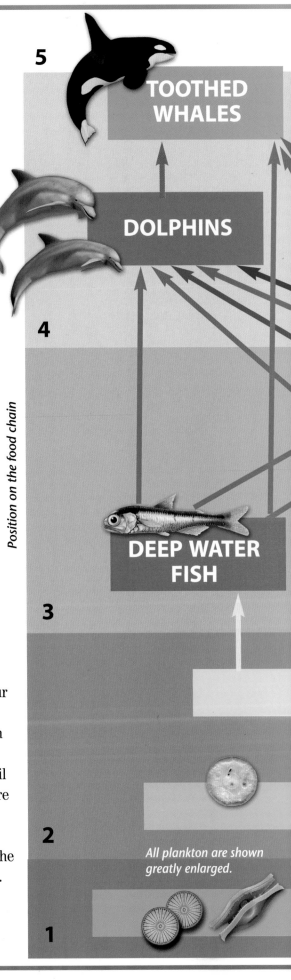

5

TOOTHED WHALES

DOLPHINS

4

Position on the food chain

DEEP WATER FISH

3

2

All plankton are shown greatly enlarged.

1

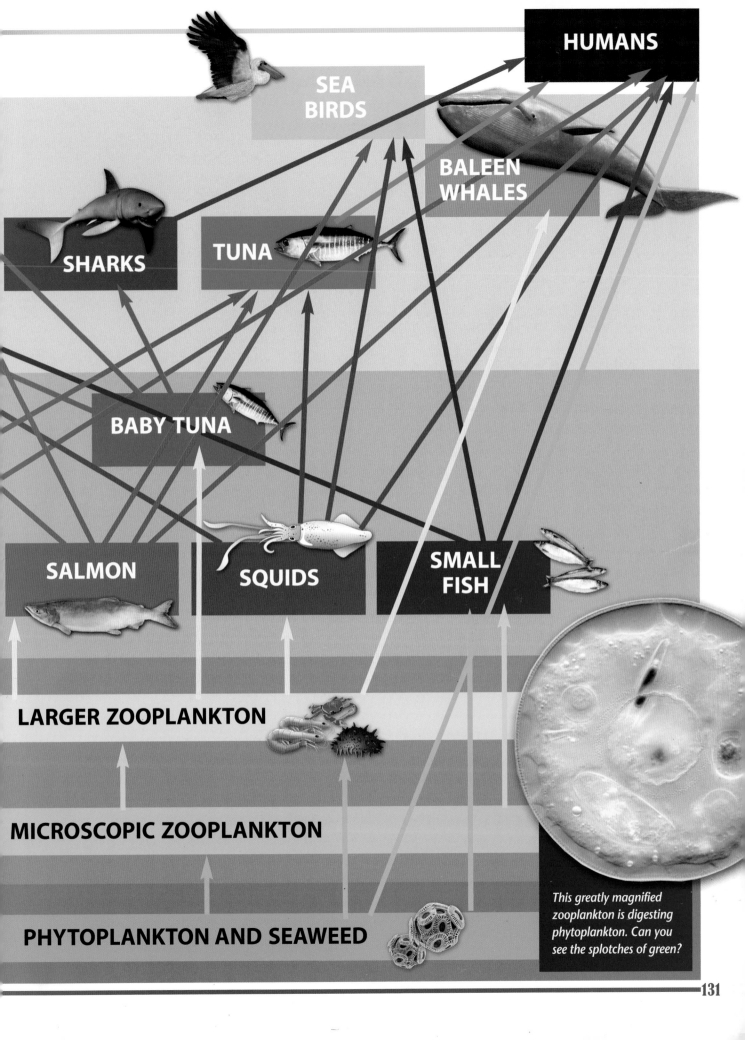

HUMANS

SEA BIRDS

BALEEN WHALES

SHARKS

TUNA

BABY TUNA

SALMON

SQUIDS

SMALL FISH

LARGER ZOOPLANKTON

MICROSCOPIC ZOOPLANKTON

PHYTOPLANKTON AND SEAWEED

This greatly magnified zooplankton is digesting phytoplankton. Can you see the splotches of green?

131

RECAP AND REVIEW

PARTS OF THE OCEAN FLOOR

Continental Shelf

Continental Slope

Continental Rise **Trench** **Abyssal Plain** **Mid-Ocean Ridge**

FOUR WAYS THE OCEAN'S WATERS MOVE

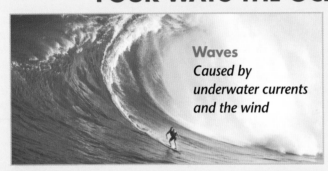

Waves
Caused by underwater currents and the wind

DANGER

STRONG CURRENT

Currents
Caused by wind patterns and differences in water density

Tides
Caused by the gravitational pull of the moon

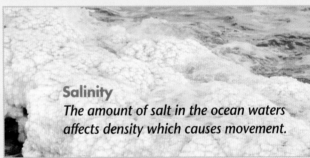

Salinity
The amount of salt in the ocean waters affects density which causes movement.

THE OCEAN'S PHYSICAL CHARACTERISTICS

Depth, salinity, and the temperature of the ocean affect where marine organisms can live.

THE BOTTOM OF THE MARINE FOOD WEB

PLANKTON

Shown greatly magnified

Phytoplankton
Tiny marine producers

Zooplankton
Tiny marine animals

Shown greatly magnified

Use pages 110-111 to answer question 1.

1. What are the three key characteristics of the ocean environment? Explain the focus of each characteristic.

Use pages 112-113 to answer question 2.

2. Describe the scientifically accepted theory of how Earth's oceans were formed.

Use pages 116-117 to answer questions 3 and 4.

3. Sketch a model of the ocean floor and label each of the major features.

4. Create a chart to show the difference in depths and features associated with each section of the ocean floor.

Use pages 118-119 to answer questions 5-7.

5. What is a current and how is it formed?

6. Explain where the Gulf Stream is located, using the globe on page 118 and the map on page 119.

7. Why do currents change in temperature as they travel through the ocean?

Use pages 120-121 to answer questions 8 and 9.

8. How does salinity affect the density of water?

9. Where is the ocean water the most dense? Why? Where is it the least dense? Why?

Use pages 122-123 to answer questions 10 and 11.

10. How are waves formed? Why does the ocean have larger waves than lakes and bays?

11. Draw and label a picture explaining how ocean tides are created.

Use pages 124-125 to answer questions 12-14.

12. Compare how much light is available to the organisms living near the surface of the ocean to the amount of light on the ocean floor.

13. What happens to the water pressure as you travel toward the ocean floor?

14. What impact does the depth of the water have on the number and type of organisms that can survive?

Use page 126 to answer question 15.

15. What is the biggest physical difference between the invertebrates and vertebrates shown on the page?

Use pages 128-129 to answer questions 16 and 17.

16. Name the two plankton classification groups. Describe the differences between the two groups.

17. Explain the importance of plankton to the ocean environment.

Use pages 130-131 to answer question 18.

18. Starting at the bottom with phytoplankton and seaweed, trace three different paths up to the top of the food web.

YOU ARE THE SCIENTIST

The Nassau grouper is a fish found in the western Atlantic Ocean, Florida Keys, Gulf of Mexico, and Caribbean Sea. It is close to extinction and is now a protected species. Hypothesize what would happen to the marine food web, the ocean environment, and humans if people continue to overfish endangered species.

DATA DETETCTIVE

Analyze the data presented. Is there a trend? What can you predict will happen in the future?

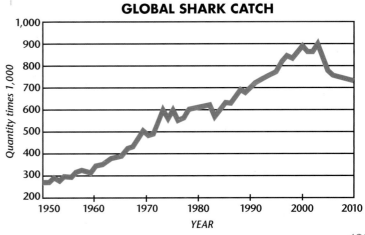

GLOBAL SHARK CATCH

Hawaii, our 50th state, has many volcanoes. Some are extinct. Some are dormant, quiet for the time being. Others, like this one, spew lava—red hot, liquid rock—from deep within the Earth.

CHAPTER SEVEN

OUR CHANGING EARTH

A fossilized trilobite. These sea-dwellers appeared more than 500 million years ago, thrived, and then became extinct before the dinosaurs.

Rocks tell many stories, but none are tall tales. Much of the story of our planet is trapped between the Earth's crustal layers. It is a story of violent explosions, crashing upheavals, and other changes in a never-ending cycle. It is a story of wild winds, blistering heat, and frigid cold. Dig deep beneath the Earth's surface to see how the story unfolds.

SECRETS OF THE EARTH

In 2000, a group of miners working 300 meters down in a silver and lead mine in Mexico found themselves gazing awestruck at a startling sight. Giant crystals, some over 11 meters long, shimmered in the dim light of their headlamps.

It was suffocatingly hot in the cave—50°C—and yet the beauty of the cave made them almost forget about the heat. They called their discovery the Cave of Crystals, and today scientists brave the difficult conditions to explore it.

These mammoth crystals formed over a period of half a million years in super-hot water, rich with minerals. The story of these huge crystals is just one chapter in the amazing saga of our planet.

EARTH GONE WILD

Our planet is constantly changing. Right under your feet, right this very second, the Earth is on the move. With every breeze, every rainfall, and every rumble deep beneath the surface, nature is hard at work carving canyons and making mountains.

You might think that rocks just lie there and don't do much of anything, but there is a lot of excitement involved in the "life" of a rock.

Some rocks are nature's storytellers and reveal events that took place billions of years ago. Some hold the trapped remains of creatures that have been extinct for eons, allowing us to see what they might have looked like. Some rocks are the product of violent explosions or fiery ruptures. Some are worth a king's fortune in gold, and some rocks actually <u>contain</u> gold.

A RAINBOW OF ROCKS

Do you think all rocks are gray, brown, or beige? Minerals, the ingredients that make up rocks, come in all sorts of colors based on the elements that are in them. The element copper helps to make some minerals more blue and green, while iron gives amethyst its purple color. Some minerals even glow under ultraviolet light.

SCIENTISTS IN THE SPOTLIGHT: EXTREME GEOLOGISTS

*From dark caves to dangerous mountain peaks, from steep canyons to icy cliffs, **geologists** (gee-ol-ah-jists) study the Earth's physical structure, its rocks, its history, and all the events that help shape it. Because they study the physical earth, their work frequently takes them to some very thrilling places. This scientist specializes in the study of volcanoes and is collecting samples of red-hot lava.*

LET'S ROCK!

Every rock on Earth is constantly moving and changing over time. Heat from deep within the Earth's core is one big reason for the changes. Wind, rain, freezing, and thawing bring even more change. All living things—including humans, of course—are responsible for many changes all around the globe. So let's grab our miners' helmets and rock-climbing gear and set off to explore our ever-changing Earth.

MARBLES FOR GIANTS?

The amazing Moeraki Boulders in New Zealand are almost perfectly round. The largest ones are as big as an elephant!

EARTH WORDS

Let's talk about the planet and the way it is constantly moving and changing.

You might look at this picture and see a gutsy adventurer scaling a cliff. Earth scientists look at this picture and see millions of years of the Earth at work—crashing, colliding, boiling, freezing, and constantly being worn away by the never-ending forces of nature.

SECRETS IN THE STONES

What kind of rock is this man climbing? Earth scientists have developed a classification system to talk about the Earth's different rocks. An earth scientist can tell you what happened a million years ago to form them. How did the cliff take shape? What caused it to have all those pits? The answers can be discovered by looking at what is happening, right this very second, beneath the Earth's surface.

HOLD ON TIGHT!
A climber clings to a steep, rock face in the HIdden Valley area of Joshua Tree National Park in California.

138

KEY WORDS TO KNOW

SEDIMENTARY ROCK
(sed-ah-men-tah-ree)
Rocks that form when small pieces are compressed together into layers. They often contain fossils.

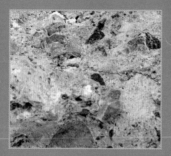

IGNEOUS ROCK
(ig-nee-us)
Rocks that form when hot magma or lava cool and harden.

METAMORPHIC ROCK
(met-ah-mor-fick)
Rocks that are changed by heat and pressure into a new rock.

WEATHERING
The breaking up of rock by water, plants, and animals.

EROSION
The movement of rock by wind and water.

DEPOSITION
(dep-uh-zi-shun)
The process by which eroded sediment is deposited and added to a landform.

DIVERGENT BOUNDARY
(die-vur-jint)
A place where the Earth's plates are drifting apart.

CONVERGENT BOUNDARY
(cun-vur-jint)
A place where the Earth's plates are pushing against each other.

TRANSFORM BOUNDARY
(trans-form)
A place where the Earth's plates slide side-by-side.

Have you ever really thought about what makes a rock a rock? Let's find out!

WHAT EXACTLY IS A ROCK?

Think about the Queen of England's crown—some velvet, a little fur and a bunch of sparkling gems. But what are those dazzling stones? What do they have to do with rocks?

HER MAJESTY'S MINERALS

A rock is not a pure substance. It is a mixture of **minerals**. If you were to slice a rock in half, you would find many minerals mixed together. Minerals are solid, crystalline (their atoms arranged in regular, geometric patterns), and nonliving. Most of the minerals we find come from the first layer of Earth, called the crust. Minerals are made from one or more elements that have been chemically combined into a compound. Remember: A compound is made of two or more elements bonded together. Elements and compounds are pure substances. So, minerals are pure substances too.

Each mineral has a slightly different chemical recipe. For example, gold is made of just gold atoms. Diamonds are made of carbon atoms. Other minerals are made of more than one element. For example, rubies have bits of aluminum, oxygen, and chromium. If you were to slice into a mineral and keep cutting it until you got to the tiniest part (an atom if the mineral was an element), or a molecule (if the mineral were made of two or more elements) you would still find only that pure mineral. So remember: A mineral is a pure substance and a rock is a mixture of minerals!

CASE STUDY:
Using cookies to understand rocks

Your favorite cookies have a lot in common with rocks. Cookies have several ingredients, depending on what kind you are making. Rocks are similar. They are made of different minerals.

1. What are the ingredients?

Every good cookie starts with a recipe. You might need sugar, butter, eggs, chocolate chips, raisins, nuts, and flour. Rocks have ingredients too, but instead of oatmeal or butterscotch morsels, they have minerals—lots of different combinations and kinds.

2. What's the recipe?

What's your favorite cookie recipe? What would happen if you added more nuts or less sugar? You'd end up with a different-tasting cookie. Rocks are the same. Depending on the quantity of minerals in each rock, you will have a different kind of rock.

3. How are you baking them?

There is one last thing to consider. If you burn your cookies or take them out of the oven before they are done, you will end up with a very different cookie than one baked at the perfect time and temperature. And guess what! Many rocks are the same. Depending on the way they were formed—in hot volcanoes, deep in the Earth's crust, pounded by the oceans—you will end up with a different rock every time. Just as no two cookies are exactly alike, no two rocks are either.

RARE AND RICH

How many minerals does it take to make a rock? There are more than 3,000 known minerals on Earth and all rocks are made up of combinations of minerals, volcanic glass, older rock fragments, fossils, or plant matter. Combinations of these minerals are what makes rocks reddish in color (lots of iron) or milky white (lots of quartz) or sparkly (lots of mica).

Some minerals are incredibly valuable because they are rare and useful. Platinum, gold, and silver are used to make electronic devices. These metallic elements are difficult to find—and can be expensive as a result. Other minerals, such as diamonds, rubies, and emeralds don't look like much until they are cut and polished. Not all minerals are rare. Take talc for example. It's used to make baby powder. Mica is ground up into eyeshadow. The value of a mineral depends on how much of it there is in the world and how hard it is to get.

JUST ROCKS?
Not exactly. These minerals are raw emeralds and rubies.

PRECIOUS GEMS
This emerald and ruby were once just stones like the ones in the bowls at the top of this page until they were cut and polished.

FROM A MINERAL TO A ROCK

Every mountain, every boulder, every pebble lying in a stream is made from combinations of different minerals. How does a mineral become a part of a rock? There are three different kinds of rock: **sedimentary, igneous,** and **metamorphic** rock. How these rocks form give us a clue as to how the minerals mixed together.

"RECIPES" FOR ROCKS

The three kinds of rock are formed in three unique ways.

SEDIMENTARY ROCK

1. Start with ANY rock.
2. Use wind, water, or natural chemicals to break the rock down into small pieces called sediments.
3. Move these sediments and allow them to pile up into layers.
4. Cement the layers together.
5. You now have a sedimentary rock!

IGNEOUS ROCK

1. Start with ANY rock.
2. Use Earth's intense heat to melt the rock into a thick liquid.
3. Allow the liquid to cool back into a solid.
4. You now have an igneous rock!

METAMORPHIC ROCK

1. Start with ANY rock.
2. Expose the rock to Earth's great heat and pressure deep in the crust.
3. Let the weight of the Earth press down really hard, and wait for the minerals that make up the rock to change shape.
4. You now have a metamorphic rock!

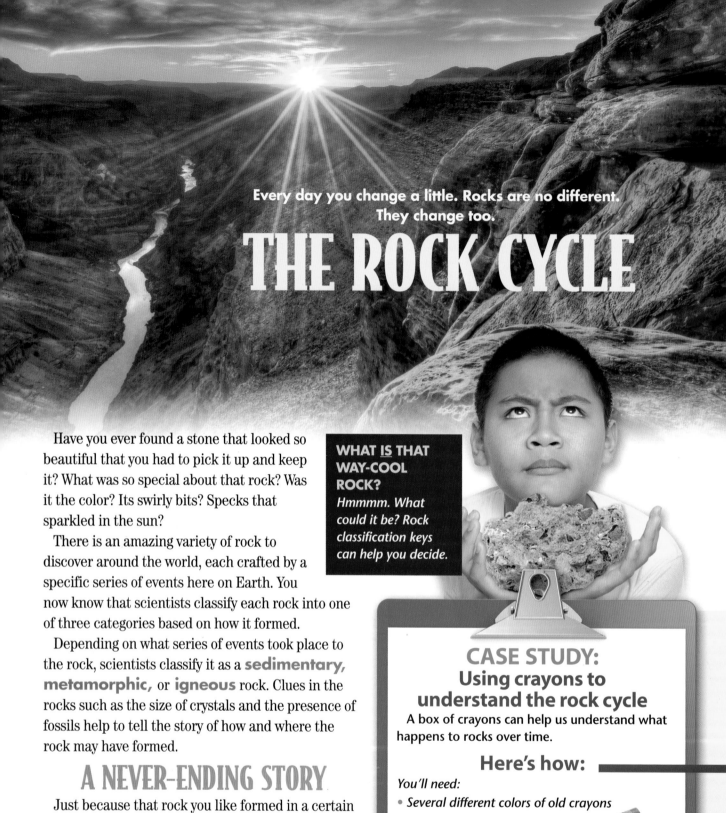

Every day you change a little. Rocks are no different.
They change too.

THE ROCK CYCLE

Have you ever found a stone that looked so beautiful that you had to pick it up and keep it? What was so special about that rock? Was it the color? Its swirly bits? Specks that sparkled in the sun?

There is an amazing variety of rock to discover around the world, each crafted by a specific series of events here on Earth. You now know that scientists classify each rock into one of three categories based on how it formed.

Depending on what series of events took place to the rock, scientists classify it as a **sedimentary, metamorphic,** or **igneous** rock. Clues in the rocks such as the size of crystals and the presence of fossils help to tell the story of how and where the rock may have formed.

A NEVER-ENDING STORY

Just because that rock you like formed in a certain way does not mean that its story is over. The Earth's surface is constantly changing. Processes such as weathering, erosion, cooling, and melting are always occurring somewhere. Any kind of rock, if it goes through the right process, can become another kind of rock, again, and again, and again! Because a rock never stops changing, these processes together are called the **rock cycle**.

WHAT IS THAT WAY-COOL ROCK?
Hmmmm. What could it be? Rock classification keys can help you decide.

CASE STUDY:
Using crayons to understand the rock cycle

A box of crayons can help us understand what happens to rocks over time.

Here's how:

You'll need:
- *Several different colors of old crayons*
- *A crayon sharpener or pair of safety scissors*
- *2 small zip-top baggies*
- *A hair dryer*

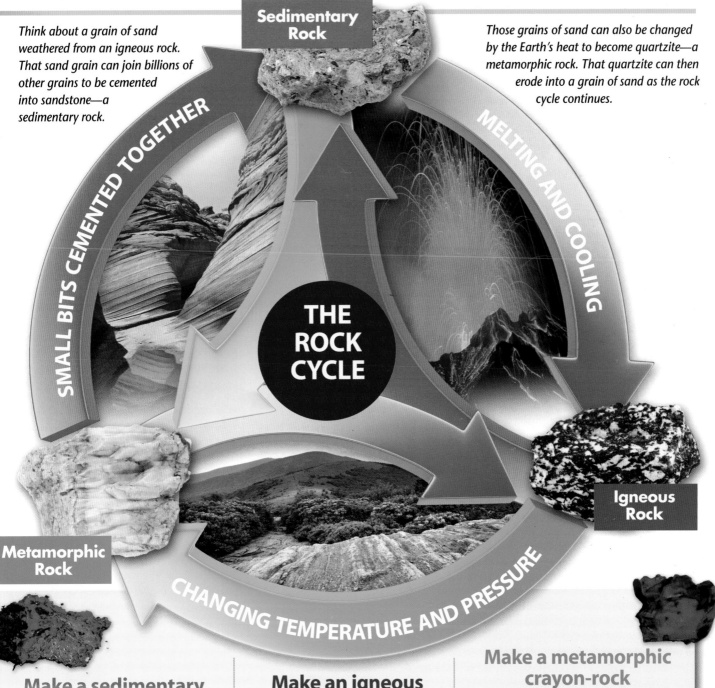

Think about a grain of sand weathered from an igneous rock. That sand grain can join billions of other grains to be cemented into sandstone—a sedimentary rock.

Those grains of sand can also be changed by the Earth's heat to become quartzite—a metamorphic rock. That quartzite can then erode into a grain of sand as the rock cycle continues.

Sedimentary Rock

SMALL BITS CEMENTED TOGETHER

MELTING AND COOLING

THE ROCK CYCLE

Metamorphic Rock

Igneous Rock

CHANGING TEMPERATURE AND PRESSURE

Make a sedimentary crayon-rock

1. Take three crayons of different colors.
2. Use the side of your scissors to scrape little bits of crayon onto a piece of paper.
3. When you have about a half cup of crayon shavings, pour them into a plastic baggie. Release all the air and seal the baggie.
4. Now stand on top of the baggie. You might even jump up and down. Your "sediments" will get stuck together.
5. That's how a sedimentary rock forms.

Make an igneous crayon-rock

1. Choose three different crayons.
2. Use the side of your scissors to scrape little bits of crayon onto a piece of paper.
3. When you have about a half cup of crayon shavings, lightly press the crayon bits into a ball and put it on a piece of paper.
4. *Aim a hairdryer at the ball until it melts into one lump.
5. That's how an igneous rock forms.

Make a metamorphic crayon-rock

1. Take three crayons of different colors.
2. Use the side of your scissors to scrape little bits of crayon onto a piece of paper.
3. When you have about a half cup of crayon shavings, pour them into a plastic baggie and zip it shut.
4. Now rub your hands together to create friction and warm them up. Squeeze the baggie for five minutes as hard as you can so that the heat of your hands presses the crayon bits together.
5. That's how a metamorphic rock forms.

Have a grown-up help you with this step.

IDENTIFYING ROCKS

What <u>is</u> that rock? How was it formed? Look for clues to figure it out.

Some of the world's oldest rocks are in Shenandoah National Park. They are made of **gneiss** *(nice)* that was formed about one billion years ago when parts of the Earth's crust collided and formed the Appalachian Mountains. What was once an igneous rock called **granite**, turned into metamorphic rock—gneiss— when the crystals were squeezed and flattened under great force and heat.

To better understand the Earth's rocks, scientists use **rock classification keys** to sort every stone on Earth into a category that explains how it forms.

CASE STUDY:
Sedimentary Rock: Cemented Together

Have you ever wiggled your toes in the sand at the beach? You're experiencing the sand early in its path to becoming a sedimentary rock. Each of those pieces of sand came from the weathering and erosion of larger rocks, possibly miles away.

The sand is considered sediment, and it collects near waterways and beaches. As layers of sand, silt, and mud pile up on top of each other, they can become compressed and cemented together to form hard, sedimentary rock. Any remains of organisms stuck in the mud may be visible as fossils in the hardened rock too.

COAL: *Compressed layers of decayed plant material*

SANDSTONE: *Cemented layers of sand grains*

LIMESTONE: *Layers of shells and marine animals*

SHALE: *Compressed, hardened layers of mud and silt*

CASE STUDY:
Igneous Rock: Melted Together

In some places in the Earth's crust, especially near volcanoes, rock gets heated so much that it melts. Melted rock is known as lava or magma depending on where it is located. On the surface of the Earth, it is called lava. When it is below the surface of the Earth, it is called magma.

Crystals form as the melted rock cools and hardens to make an igneous rock. Small or invisible crystals suggest that the rock cooled quickly. Large crystals indicate the rock cooled slowly—REALLY slowly—over a period of thousands to millions of years, giving the crystals time to develop.

GRANITE: *Slowly cooled magma forms big crystals.*

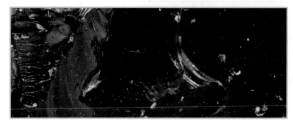

OBSIDIAN: *Quickly cooled lava forms a natural glass.*

CASE STUDY:
Metamorphic Rock: Heated and Squeezed Together

Deep within the Earth's crust, there are some places where there is enough heat and pressure to chemically change rocks. As these rocks get heated and squeezed, the crystals that make up the original rock change into something new.

Limestone becomes marble

Shale becomes slate

GNEISS: *Granite's crystals now appear wavy.*

SLATE: *Flaky, compressed shale becomes hard slate.*

If you find an awesome rock, ask yourself lots of questions as you study it closely. It helps to have a rock I.D. kit with:
- *notebook and colored pencils*
- *magnifying glass* • *ruler*
- *an old, heavy drinking glass*
- *a small plastic bottle of vinegar*
- *an eyedropper*

BE A ROCK DETECTIVE!

Scientists sort rocks based on many different characteristics. It is important to make close observations and record your thinking.

1. *Select a rock to study. Measure its length, width, and depth.*

2. *Draw a sketch of the rock and make a note of its color.*

3. *Are there visible grains? Can you see any with a magnifying glass? If you can see grains, be sure to add them to your picture. Try to accurately draw the shape and size of the grains.*

4. *Do you see layers? If you can see layers, add them to your picture.*

5. *Is the rock hard or soft? Test this by using the rock to make a 1 cm scratch on the glass. If the rock is hard, it will scratch the glass. Make sure it has actually left a groove and not just a film of grit.*

6. *Does the rock react with an acid? Put a 10 ml drop of vinegar on the rock and see if it starts to fizz. Limestone and marble are two rocks that will react to acid. What did your rock do?*

Whdt do rocks and fossils have to do with each other?

FOSSILS

SPEAK LIKE A SCIENTIST

Fossil

(fah-sill)

The preserved remains or imprints of animals, plants, and other organisms from the distant past.

Historians use many clues to discover long-ago cultures. In Jamestown, Virginia, for example, archeologists have uncovered old buildings, skeletons, and artifacts. Each of these discoveries provides hints as to what life was like in the settlement 400 years ago.

The buildings in Jamestown might be old, but the rocks they are built upon are much, much older. Some Virginia rocks are more than a million times older than the buildings. Scientists study the history of the Earth, trying to figure out what the landscape looked like and what creatures roamed across the continent long before Jamestown ever existed. What did the land look like one thousand years ago? One million years ago? One billion years ago? Fossils are kind of like "photos" of long-ago times.

THE STORIES ROCKS TELL

Like cookies, rocks are different depending on the ingredients and conditions under which they are made. If you end up with a gooey oatmeal-raisin cookie, you know that there must have been oatmeal and raisins in the kitchen when the cookies were made. In the same way, if you discover a layer of sedimentary rock that has imprints of shells and other marine creatures, then you know that the land was once underwater.

DINOSAURS IN VIRGINIA
Thousands of dinosaur footprints solidified in rock have been discovered across Northern Virginia. This man shows a dinosaur footprint fossil he discovered in Gainesville.

OUR STATE FOSSIL
This fossilized scallop shell, Chesapecten jeffersonius, is named in honor of Thomas Jefferson. The creature that created this fossil lived about 4.5 million years ago. This species is now extinct, but fossils of it can currently be found along many stream beds in southeastern Virginia.

As scientists gather and share clues about what they have uncovered, the story of the Earth starts to unfold. Even when they think they have a pretty good idea of what happened in an area, they never stop looking for more clues. As they collect more evidence, they constantly improve their understanding of the saga of our planet.

146

HOW A FOSSIL FORMS

If you find a fossil, you are most likely looking at a sedimentary rock. Fossils form when the remains of a living organism are trapped within layers of sediment.

1. *This dinosaur has just died. Its body begins to press into the soil.*

2. *After just a few months only the bones remain. Water seeps into the bones, carrying minerals from the soil that bond with the bones.*

3. *Over many thousands of years, layer upon layer of sediment will cover the remains.*

4. *Many thousands of years later, erosion will wear away the Earth's layers, revealing the fossil.*

VIRGINIA'S FOSSIL STORY

Virginia's story starts about one billion years ago when two different pieces of the Earth's crust collided. Pressure and heat from the collision created the metamorphic rocks that are buried deep in the layers of the Blue Ridge Mountains. Since then, the land has moved a lot. It separated to form an ancient ocean, then moved back together to form more mountains, and finally moved apart again to form the present Atlantic Ocean. How do scientists know this? They look at rocks!

This five foot long fossil of an ancient whale skull was found along the Virginia shore after a huge hurricane washed away rock and sand.

Rocks in the Coastal Plain/Tidewater region of Virginia contain bones and teeth from ancient ocean animals. This tells us that the area was once covered by an ocean. Shells of snails and clams have been found in the rocks here, as well as whale bones and shark teeth.

DINOSAURS!

Farther inland, in the Piedmont region of Virginia, thousands of fossilized dinosaur footprints have been found. This means that about 150 million years ago, dinosaurs were dwelling all across the region. Much later, other now extinct animals, like mastodons and giant ground sloths, also left their marks on Virginia's rocks. The proof is in the fossils.

A cast of a dinosaur footprint, found in the Piedmont.

SURPRISES IN THE COAL

The coal in the Appalachian Mountains is a clue that this region was once a swampy coastal area, full of many trees and gigantic ferns. It was once warm and steamy, like the Florida Everglades today. Those giant plants eventually died and fell to the bottom of the swamp, slowly becoming coal. How do we know this? Sometimes you can find an imprint of a fern in a piece of coal. Now *that's* a fossil fuel!

LAYERS OF THE EARTH

You've heard of layered cake. Now dig in to layered Earth.

Think about how deep Virginia's coal mines are. Are they close to the center of the Earth? No way! Virginia's deepest mine shaft—the Buchanan Mine in Buchanan County, is about 605 m deep. The deepest mine in the world is 3.9 km deep. You would have to drill another 6,374 km through several layers to reach the Earth's center. Earth has four major layers: **crust, mantle, outer core,** and **inner core**.

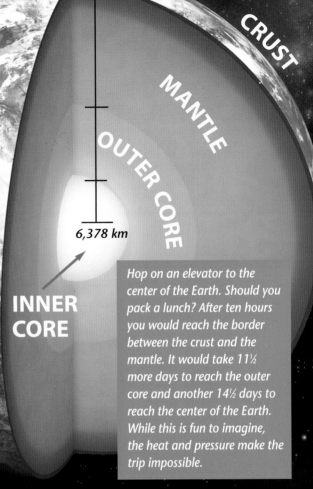

CRUST

MANTLE

OUTER CORE

6,378 km

INNER CORE

Hop on an elevator to the center of the Earth. Should you pack a lunch? After ten hours you would reach the border between the crust and the mantle. It would take 11½ more days to reach the outer core and another 14½ days to reach the center of the Earth. While this is fun to imagine, the heat and pressure make the trip impossible.

THE CRUST

Look outside your window. The hard rock just beneath the soil is the crust. The crust is Earth's thinnest layer—anywhere from 5 to 70 km thick. Our homes and schools are built on top of the crust. Even the oceans sit on the crust. Powerful forces deep inside the Earth have broken the crust into many pieces called **tectonic plates**.

THE MANTLE

Just as an eggshell sits on top of the egg, the Earth's crust actually floats on top of the mantle. The mantle is Earth's thickest layer and much hotter than the crust. Heat from even deeper inside the Earth makes the mantle move like a very thick liquid. Even though the mantle is a solid, it still moves a few centimeters a year because of all the heat. The movement in the mantle breaks the crust up into the tectonic plates. As these plates drift on the moving mantle, they sometimes crash into each other. When tectonic plates collide, split, or slide by each other we sometimes feel this as earthquakes and volcanoes.

CRACKING UP
The Earth's crust is cracked into pieces just like the shell of this hardboiled egg. The pieces can rub up against each other, collide with each other, or move apart.

DIGGING DEEP HOLES

The Buchanan Mine in Buchanan County, Virginia: deepest shaft is 605 meters deep.

TauTona Gold Mine in South Africa: deepest shaft is 3.9 km.

The deepest hole ever drilled into the Earth is in Russia: 12.2 km deep.

THE OUTER CORE

The outer core lies beneath the mantle and is made mostly of the elements iron and nickel. This liquid layer is even hotter than the mantle. It is so hot these metals have melted. The movement of the metals in this layer causes the Earth's magnetic field.

THE INNER CORE

The inner core is also made of iron and nickel and is the hottest layer in the Earth. Temperatures reach over 6,000°C. Here the metals are no longer liquid because of the intense pressure. Gravity pulls the other three layers down on top of the inner core, pressing it so hard that it becomes solid.

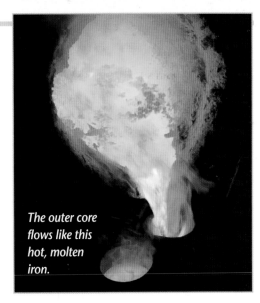

The outer core flows like this hot, molten iron.

CASE STUDY:
Layered Earth

120 ml water (colored with blue food coloring)
240 ml vegetable oil • 120 ml dish soap
1 tablespoon rubbing alcohol (colored with red food coloring) • A tall, clear glass

Why does Earth have layers?

1. Slowly pour the dish soap into the tall glass.
2. Gently tilt the glass and slowly pour the colored water so that it sits on top of the dish soap layer.
3. Slowly add the vegetable oil as the next layer.
4. Finally, add the rubbing alcohol on top.

The four layers you see in your glass are like the four layers of the Earth. They are separated because of their densities. The densest layer sinks to the bottom. Which layer in the glass represents the inner core? The outer core? The mantle? The crust? What can you conclude about the densities of the layers?

EARTH'S ENGINE

It is amazing to think that forces hundreds of kilometers deep within the Earth cause changes here on the surface. The heat from the core and the moving mantle are responsible for the sliding tectonic plates. Mountains, volcanoes, and earthquakes occur when these plates interact—pushing together, pulling apart, or sliding next to each other.

We can thank Earth's mighty internal engine for Virginia's Appalachian Mountains. About 480 million years ago two tectonic plates collided and pushed those mountains upward.

A satellite view shows the Appalachians where two plates collided.

SCIENTISTS IN THE SPOTLIGHT: LIFE IN THE LAYERS

Would it surprise you to hear that perhaps half the living organisms on Earth may live thousands of meters underground? Microbiologists have discovered all sorts of life forms living so deep down that they have no contact with anything touched by the sun. These microbes have been called "the toughest organisms on the planet."

The microbes thrive in a place where the water is full of acids, sometimes boiling hot, or as solidly frozen as the Antarctic. Amazingly, some microbes might even live to be a thousand years old.

How do you study these creatures? The two scientists on the left are working 3.5 km underground in a tunnel drilled deep into the Earth. Their findings raise an important question: Could microbial life exist beneath the surfaces of other planets or their moons? What do you think?

149

EARTH'S PUZZLE PIECES

You have fire drills. In some states in America, kids also have earthquake and volcano drills!

Just outside of Seattle, Washington, there is a very beautiful, potentially dangerous mountain. Scientists study it constantly so that they can warn people in the nearby city before trouble arises. Why? Mt. Rainier is an active volcano.

In California, students routinely crawl under their desks to practice earthquake drills. In that region there are dozens of earthquakes every day that are too small for people to feel but every once in a while, one will be big enough to make everything shake and roll. Here in Virginia we are a lot safer, but in 2011, a rare, large earthquake toppled merchandise from store shelves and cracked walls. *What* on earth is going on with Earth?

Mt. Rainier ⟶

CRACKS IN THE CRUST

While we have occasional small earthquakes here on the east coast of the United States, we don't have nearly as many as there are in other parts of the world. The reason for this lies deep within the Earth. If you've ever baked a cherry pie, you will know that the gooey inner part bubbles and boils as it cooks. This movement sometimes causes the crust to bend and crack. Sometimes some of the sticky goo oozes out above the crust. Keep this sweet image in your mind as you think about what's happening to our planet.

ON THE MOVE
Continent-size blocks of crust move slowly because of constant movement in the mantle. Sometimes these blocks crash into each other. Sometimes they grind alongside each other. And sometimes, they pull apart with fiery results!

CONVERGENT BOUNDARY

DIVERGENT BOUNDARY

OCEAN-CONTINENT CONVERGENT BOUNDARY

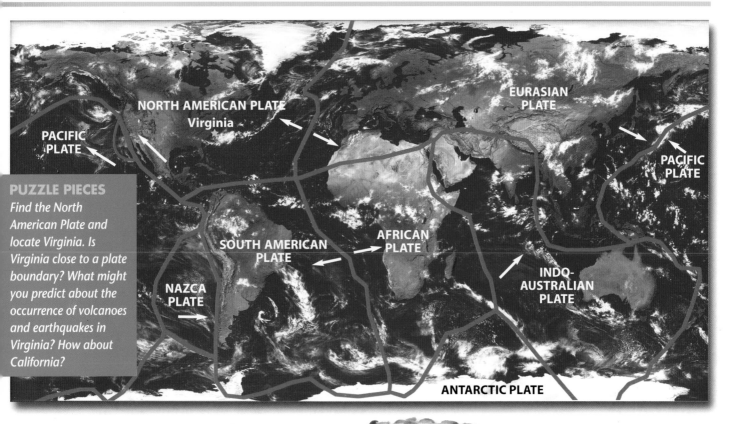

NORTH AMERICAN PLATE
Virginia

EURASIAN PLATE

PACIFIC PLATE

PACIFIC PLATE

PUZZLE PIECES
Find the North American Plate and locate Virginia. Is Virginia close to a plate boundary? What might you predict about the occurrence of volcanoes and earthquakes in Virginia? How about California?

SOUTH AMERICAN PLATE

AFRICAN PLATE

NAZCA PLATE

INDO-AUSTRALIAN PLATE

ANTARCTIC PLATE

OOZY AND GOOEY

Thermal (heat) energy within the Earth's core moves the mantle slowly, sort of like the cherry goo in a hot pie. The hot inner rock of the Earth's mantle rises toward the crust when it is heated and sinks back down when it cools. Since the crust sits on the mantle, it is actually floating on that hot, moving rock (like your pie crust sits on the hot fruity mixture). The movement pushes and pulls on the Earth's crust causing it to break into many large, drifting pieces called **tectonic plates**. These tectonic plates are bigger than continents because most tectonic plates also include crust found under oceans.

Why does Virginia only have small earthquakes and no volcanoes? Most big earthquakes and volcanoes occur very close to the edges of the tectonic plates. California and Washington state are both on the edge of a plate, while Virginia is thousands of kilometers away from a plate edge.

ON THE EDGE

The edges of tectonic plates are known as **plate boundaries**. Plates move in very specific directions depending on the direction of the mantle below them. The arrows on the above map show the direction each plate moves. There are three main types of plate boundaries: **divergent, convergent,** and **transform**. Scientists look at patterns in the locations of earthquakes and volcanoes to find out where these boundaries are on the Earth.

A RING OF FIRE

If you look at the map below, you will notice that a lot of volcanoes are located along the edge of the Pacific Ocean. For this reason, the area has earned the nickname "the Ring of Fire." Seventy-five percent of the Earth's land volcanoes are in this region—over 450 volcanoes, stretching over 40,000 km in length. As you can see, some of the United States is a part of this ring.

ASIA
Aleutian trench
Kurile trench
Japan trench
Izu Bonin trench
Ryukyu trench
Philippine trench
Marianas trench
Challenger Deep
Bougainville trench
Java (Sunda) trench
Tonga trench
Kermadec trench
AUSTRALIA
NORTH AMERICA
Pacific Ocean
Middle America trench
Equator
Peru-Chile trench

A group of volcanoes in Java

151

WHOSE FAULT IS IT?
The San Andreas Fault runs through parts of California. Here, two plates slowly slide alongside each other, moving at about the same rate as an average person's fingernails grow.

Why has the Earth crumpled in this part of California?

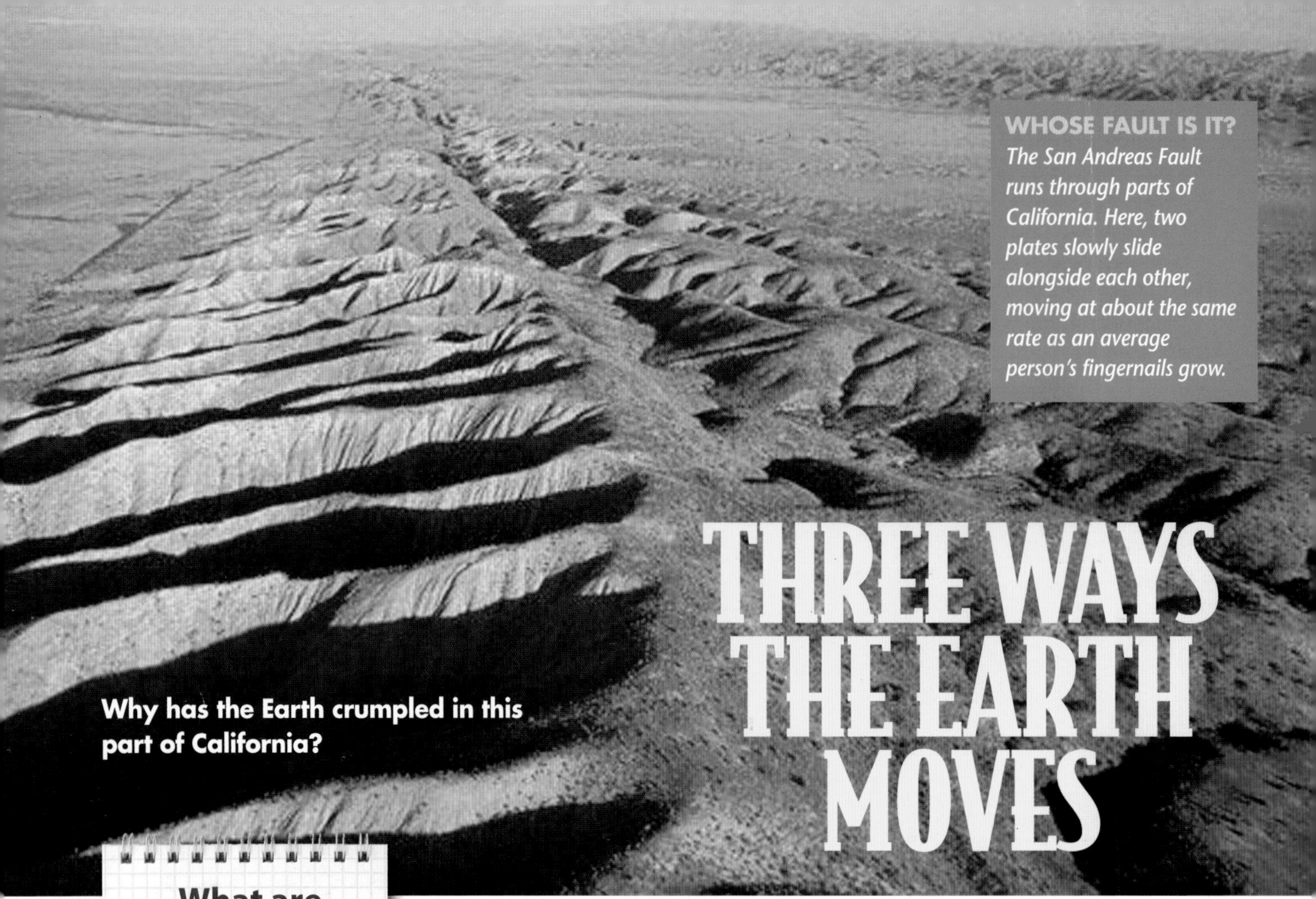

THREE WAYS THE EARTH MOVES

What are the effects of a DIVERGENT boundary?

- ☑ earthquakes
- ☑ volcanoes
- ☒ trenches
- ☒ mountains
- ☑ mid-ocean ridges

Where plates meet, action often occurs. But why are there earthquakes AND volcanoes in some places like Seattle, Washington, and just earthquakes in others? The answer lies in the direction the plates move at different boundaries.

DIVERGENT BOUNDARIES

The nearest plate boundary to Virginia is a **divergent boundary**. To diverge means to separate. At this kind of boundary, the Earth's tectonic plates are moving away from each other. As they pull apart, hot liquid rock from the mantle moves up to fill the empty space, generating new crust through volcanic eruptions.

Where is Virgina's closest plate boundary? It is deep under the Atlantic Ocean, halfway between North America and Europe. New ocean floor is actually being created along this plate boundary. In fact, a chain of volcanic mountains has grown in the middle of the Atlantic Ocean. Together they are known as the Mid-Atlantic Ridge. Many small earthquakes occur here as well, but we don't notice them in Virginia because we are too far away.

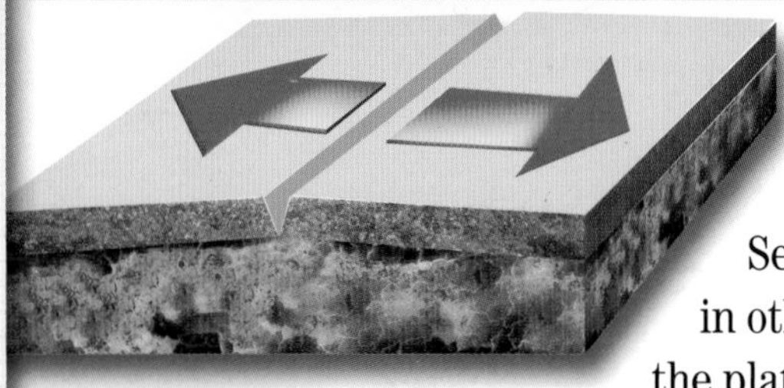

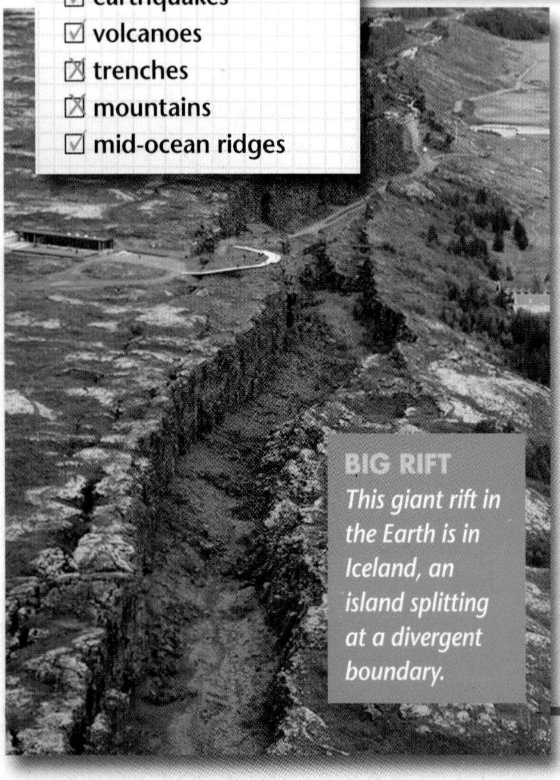

BIG RIFT
This giant rift in the Earth is in Iceland, an island splitting at a divergent boundary.

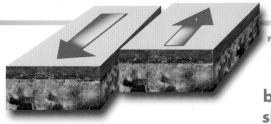

TRANSFORM BOUNDARIES

California is located on a **transform boundary**—sometimes called a **strike-slip** or **sliding boundary**. These plates do not slide easily alongside each other. When they get stuck, it creates friction. The energy that builds up is finally released as an earthquake. Areas like this have tiny earthquakes every day. Few of them are strong enough to be felt by humans, and even fewer are strong enough to cause damage to roads and buildings.

Some people think that Los Angeles will break off and fall into the ocean, but now that you know California is on a transform boundary, you can see that is not possible. If plates continue moving on their current paths, the land around Los Angeles will just keep sliding northwest a few centimeters a year toward San Francisco. Maybe someday, millions of years from now, it might be easy to walk between the two cities!

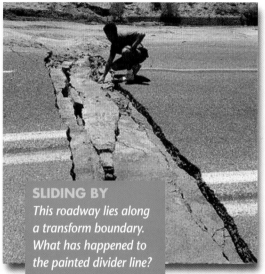

SLIDING BY
This roadway lies along a transform boundary. What has happened to the painted divider line?

What are the effects of a TRANSFORM boundary?

- ☑ earthquakes
- ☒ volcanoes
- ☒ trenches
- ☒ mountains
- ☒ mid-ocean ridges

CONVERGENT BOUNDARIES

To converge means to come together. **Convergent boundaries** happen where the tectonic plates are moving toward each other. Imagine a car crash in very, *v-e-r-y* slow motion. Now, picture two huge chunks of the Earth doing the same thing. Where they crash, the surface of Earth changes drastically!

There are different types of convergent boundaries. In one type, continental plates crash directly into each other, causing earthquakes and forming mountain ranges. The Himalaya mountains (shown below) grow several centimeters each year as the Indo-Australian Plate keeps crashing into the Eurasian Plate. Here in the United States, in Oregon, the edge of the ocean plate keeps sinking beneath the continental plate. The ocean plate melts back into the mantle and is recycled. Either way, the surface of the Earth keeps changing.

What are the effects of a CONVERGENT boundary?

- ☑ earthquakes
- ☑ volcanoes
- ☑ trenches
- ☑ mountains
- ☒ mid-ocean ridges

EARTH'S NEWEST MOUNTAINS
Mt. Everest is the highest peak on Earth. It is still growing even higher.

153

Why is the ground shaking so violently?

EARTHQUAKE!

Rub your hands together. They move back and forth pretty easily, right? Earth's tectonic plates do not slide past each other as easily as this. Friction keeps them stuck in one position most of the time. But remember, the mantle is always moving underneath the plates. Force slowly builds up and the edges start to bend. Finally, at the moment when the force becomes too great, the plates suddenly give way and lurch past each other, relieving the pressure. The ground shifts quickly and a burst of energy is released. This release of energy is an **earthquake**.

THE POWER TO BREAK BRIDGES

In 1989 a huge earthquake struck San Francisco, a city that is built near a plate boundary. The upper deck of the Bay Bridge collapsed and fell onto the lower deck. That quake brought $10 billion in damages.

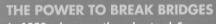

A WHOLE LOT OF SHAKING GOING ON

There are many reasons earthquakes happen around the world, but most occur near plate boundaries where the tectonic plates are rubbing against each other. Breaks in the Earth's crust where the ground moves during an earthquake are called **faults**. If a lot of energy is released, people living close to the earthquake will feel the ground shake or roll. Even though smaller earthquakes may not be noticed by humans, machines called **seismographs** (*size-mah-grafs*) can detect released energy thousands of miles away.

During an earthquake, the ground can slip along a fault anywhere from 6 mm to more than 6 meters. Japan's massive 2011 earthquake caused a fault to move upward more than 30 meters!

SPEAK LIKE A SCIENTIST

Fault
A break in the Earth's crust that results from the ground shifting.

DAMAGING ENERGY

Fault lines can exist in many places. They do not have to be near a plate boundary. The location on the surface of the Earth directly above where the earthquake starts is called the **epicenter**. Just like ripples on a pond from a tossed pebble, energy radiates outward from the fault in all directions. These waves shake the Earth as they move through it. As waves reach the Earth's surface, the ground and everything on it—including us—starts to roll and shake.

If a lot of energy is released, the area near the epicenter during an earthquake will probably experience a lot of damage to buildings, roads, and bridges. Scientists cannot yet predict when earthquakes will occur, so people who live near fault lines must make special preparations. In the United States, buildings near plate boundaries are designed to withstand the shaking. Cities in these areas also have emergency response plans in place.

EPICENTER: MINERAL, VA
Groceries tumbled from store shelves during a 5.8 earthquake in Virginia in 2011.

MEASURING EARTHQUAKES

The Richter scale is how scientists calculate how much energy is released by an earthquake. Many earthquakes occur each day around the world that have low scores (between 0 and 2.9 on this scale). Thankfully large earthquakes like the 9.0 in Japan in 2011 are very rare, occurring only every few years.

0-1.9 *Felt only by seismograph*	**4-4.9** *Windows may break*	**7-7.9** *Buildings knocked off foundations*
2-2.9 *Hanging objects may swing*	**5-5.9** *Furniture moves, walls crack*	**8-8.9** *Bridges destroyed, few structures left*
3-3.9 *Vibrations similar to a passing truck*	**6-6.9** *Damage to well-built structures*	**9 and over** *Near total destruction in quake area*

MORE ABOUT TSUNAMIS

You read about the 2011 tsunami that struck Japan, on page 123. It was caused by a huge earthquake deep beneath the Pacific Ocean along the coast of northern Japan. Underwater earthquakes can sometimes cause these destructive ocean waves, especially at convergent plate boundaries. Tsunamis are very rare because three things need to happen: The earthquake needs to occur in crust that is underwater; it needs to be very powerful; and part of the crust needs to slip in an upward motion. The slipping crust pushes up the huge mass of water sitting above it. The water then begins to move out in all directions. As the tsunami approaches the coastline, the large volume of water rushes on shore and the waves can be powerful enough to knock over trees, destroy buildings, and even push big ships onto building rooftops!

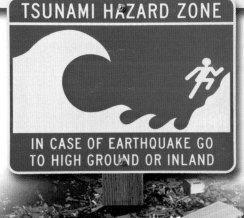

TSUNAMI HAZARD ZONE

IN CASE OF EARTHQUAKE GO TO HIGH GROUND OR INLAND

VOLCANO!

With a rumble and a grumble, the Earth spits and spews fiery rock.

Volcanoes occur all around the globe, mostly near plate boundaries. Often we think of them in tropical areas like Hawaii, but there are many volcanoes in icy Alaska and other cold climates too. A volcano buried deep beneath a glacier can still erupt.

The tectonic plates of the Earth's crust move on the mantle layer underneath. As one plate slides under the other, it starts to melt, forming magma that erupts onto the surface

Volcano

Ocean

Trench

Continental Crust

Mantle

FEELING HOT-HOT-HOT

At convergent boundaries, volcanoes occur when an ocean plate sinks beneath another plate. As the ocean plate moves into the mantle, some of the rock melts and rises up through the crust. This hot, melted rock, called **magma**, can force its way explosively out of the crust or run in slow, orange rivers of liquid rock. Once the melted rock is on the surface, it is called **lava**.

ANOTHER WAY TO EXPLODE

At divergent boundaries, plates move away from each other and magma rises from within the mantle, filling the crack left by the separating plates. This often forms long underwater mountain chains called mid-ocean ridges. Ridges like this run for thousands of miles in every ocean. If you were to explore the bottom of the Atlantic Ocean, you'd find a huge volcanic mountain chain running right down the middle!

A Mid-Ocean Ridge

WITH A BIG BANG

Volcanic eruptions cause big changes. What was once flat land can become a huge volcano. Eruptions force magma and rock onto the surface of the Earth, resulting in a growing mound of lava and rock that can eventually be thousands of meters high. Most volcanic eruptions happen with a BANG! These violent eruptions release so much pressure that part of the volcano explodes, blasting rock into tiny pieces called ash. The ash falls on nearby areas, blanketing cars, houses, and the land like snow. This ash can be dangerous to breathe and if enough of the ash compacts, it can even crush buildings. But in time, it also will create very fertile soil for growing plants, trees, and food crops.

These people are holding up a photo of Mount St. Helens in Washington state taken just before it erupted in 1980. Compare the two. Can you infer what happened to make such a big difference?

A SLOW OOZE

Some volcanoes never explode. They simply ooze lava. Homes and landscapes are sometimes burned as the lava flows over them, but because it is slower-moving, the people in the area have plenty of warning and can get to safety. Volcanoes with oozing lava leave behind fields of new rock that look like lumpy parking lots. Eventually, small plants will start to grow here and break the rock into soil, thus allowing larger plants to grow. Soon the land will be green again.

LAVA'S LEGACY
The slopes of this extinct volcano in the Caribbean are now lush and green.

LINK TO THE PAST
Pompeii
In the shadow of Mt. Vesuvius lies the haunting remains of a once-lively ancient Roman town—Pompeii.
For almost 1,700 years it lay forgotten, its citizens dead and buried under a 25-meter-thick layer of ash and pumice that covered Pompeii when Vesuvius erupted in the year 69. In the mid-1700s workmen digging a foundation discovered the long forgotten town. Since then, scientists and historians have worked together to understand what triggered the eruption and how Pompeii's people perished. They are also still uncovering the well-preserved remains of the city and trying to protect the remains for future generations.

157

There is a force hard at work, every second of every day, breaking down the landscape bit by bit.

WEATHERING

The Great Sphinx of Egypt was built to be a sign of the power of the pharaohs and Egyptian civilization. Four thousand years later, parts of this massive outdoor sculpture have worn away. Why? The Great Sphinx is made out of limestone. Even a moderately hard sedimentary rock like limestone breaks down over time. Every day, Egypt's desert environment keeps eating away at the stone. At some point in the distant future if left unrepaired, the last grains of the Sphinx will blow off with the wind and disappear.

The breaking down of rocks is called **weathering**. This can happen in many ways. Despite the name, "weather"-ing doesn't always involve the weather. Plant roots grow into rock, animals burrow in the soil, and chemical changes caused by acid rain can eat away at rocks. Weathering is always happening everywhere on Earth. The next time you walk around your neighborhood, keep your eyes peeled for signs of weathering. Is a tree root pushing up the pavement? Is there moss growing on a boulder? Be aware!

SOME WAYS ROCKS WEATHER

Water

FREEZING WATER

Water trapped in cracks in the rocks freezes in the winter. Freezing water expands with a force so great that it can break the rock.

Chemicals

SMALL PLANTS

Plants like moss "weather" rocks too. As they grow they produce small amounts of certain chemicals that slowly break the rock down into smaller pieces.

A TALE OF TWO OBELISKS

These tall monuments are made of granite, a very hard igneous rock. Even after standing in the Egyptian desert for 3,000 years, the hieroglyphs on the obelisk on the left still look as good as new. These symbols fared much better than the Sphinx's nose because of granite's hardness. So what happened to the hieroglyphs in the obelisk pictured on the right? Weathering!

That obelisk was moved to New York City as a gift from Egypt about 130 years ago. In this short time, the hieroglyphs have become unreadable. What is different about New York and Egypt? More rain falls in New York, so the rate of weathering increased greatly. The rain in the eastern United States also contains small amounts of acids that eat away at many kinds of rocks, breaking them down faster than typical rain.

CASE STUDY:
Obelisk-Away

You'll need: Sidewalk chalk, vinegar, a small cup, an eyedropper, a paper clip.

1. Unfold a paper clip so that you can carve your own hieroglyphs into the piece of chalk. Scratch your own art or words carefully onto the chalk.

2. Put a small amount of vinegar into a cup. With the eyedropper add one drop of vinegar to the chalk where you made your design. What do you observe?

3. Add more drops of vinegar to your design.

The vinegar affects the chalk in much the same way as the mild acids in New York's rain affect the granite. If you rub your finger over the place where you dropped the vinegar, you will speed up the weathering of the chalk even more.

CLAWING CRITTERS
Animals that dig burrows and tunnels are culprits when it comes to the breaking down of rock.

Wind

BLOWING GRIT
At high speeds wind can carry small bits of sand. The blowing sand chips off tiny pieces from larger rocks. Over many years, this can have a dramatic effect.

Pressure

ROOTS
As trees grow, their roots can find their way into cracks in the rock. Eventually, the growing tree roots wedge the rock apart.

EROSION AND DEPOSITION

The process of weathering breaks off pieces of larger rocks, but the story doesn't end there. In fact, it's only a beginning. The smaller pieces of weathered rock are called **sediment**. Sediment is carried away by natural forces like wind, water, ice, and gravity. The movement of sediment is called **erosion**. When the sediment finally stops moving, it gets dropped or deposited. This is called **deposition**.

THREE PROCESSES MADE SIMPLE

Imagine chipping off a small piece of a piggy bank with a hammer, and then carrying it outside and dropping it on the ground. You have weathered (broken it off), eroded (carried it away), and deposited (dropped) that piggy-piece!

The same thing happens constantly in nature to rocks all over the surface of the Earth.

A dust storm stirs sand across a roadway.

GONE WITH THE WIND?

How far will the sediment travel? How fast will it move? Where will it end up? How quickly will the moving rock break down into even smaller pieces? Answers to these questions can vary depending on the landscape and the method of erosion. In very sandy areas like beaches and deserts, the wind and waves can move the sand many kilometers. The sand often piles up in distinctive patterns known as sand dunes. In fact, dunes are always moving and changing shape because of the wind.

SAND MEETS MOUNTAINS
Great Sand Dunes National Park in Colorado is home to the tallest sand dunes in North America. Some are taller than the Washington Monument!

GRAVITY AT WORK

Just as gravity continually pulls down on us and keeps us from flying off into space, it also tugs downward on rocks. Sometimes a rock that is loose enough will be pulled down off the face of a cliff or slope, falling far below. Those falling rocks might even be smashed into smaller bits. From here, some rock pieces will be carried off by another force of erosion, such as water.

WATER AT WORK

As water moves over a surface, it can push rocks. Whether it is a trickle of water in a sluggish stream or pounding waves after an ocean storm, the force of water can erode surfaces by transporting sediment. Depending on how fast the water is moving, it can push layers of sand, large boulders, or any-sized rock in between! Sediment—matter that settles to the bottom of a liquid—can occur.

This river is full of sediment—the result of deposition.

ICE AT WORK

Glaciers are large masses of ice that slowly flow down from some mountains. As the ice moves, it carries sediment in its path and then deposits it where the ice melts. You can sometimes tell where a glacier used to be because of the piles of giant boulders strewn like enormous toy blocks all over the landscape. Sometimes enormous rocks end up in odd spots when the glacier melts away.

DID A GIANT MOVE THIS ROCK?

Large boulders that are left in odd places are called "glacial erratics" because they were deposited by melting glaciers. They are called "erratic" because these large boulders are made of rock unrelated to any nearby rocks—for example, a slab of granite sitting on a bed of sedimentary rock.

161

PUT DOWN ROOTS!
Add plants with strong roots to hillsides and slopes where the soil is eroding away. The plants' roots will help hold the soil in place and prevent more erosion.

The Earth's forces are massive and sometimes destructive, but we can still do things to help control them.

YOU AND THE EARTH

The Earth's landscape is constantly being changed because of weathering, erosion, and deposition. Sometimes change happens on a huge scale, like a big rockslide down a mountain, but other times, if you look closely, you can see small changes happening all around you.

The Earth provides us with many clues—you just need to have a sharp eye and take the time to observe. The good news is that there are many things we can do to control erosion and prevent damage from natural disasters. Why not start right now in your school or community?

CASE STUDY: Oh Weathering, Where Are You?

Start by heading outside. Walk slowly and explore the area closely. Do you see any signs of weathering?

Can you find any areas where a tree is growing too close to a sidewalk, causing it to crack?
THAT'S WEATHERING!

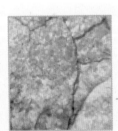

Can you find any rocks with cracks where it looks like the rock is starting to break apart?
THAT'S WEATHERING!

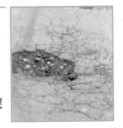

Do you see any cracks on a street or on the playground caused from water freezing?
THAT'S WEATHERING!

CASE STUDY: Erosion Is Everywhere!

Look for areas of erosion. Remember, you're trying to find places where water or wind have caused sediments to move.

Can you find places where tree roots or rocks were once buried but are now exposed?
THAT'S EROSION!

Can you find little paths in the soil where plants don't grow anymore and water has flowed?
THAT'S EROSION!

Can you find areas at the beach where sand has been washed away leaving large rocks behind
THAT'S EROSION!

If it is raining or has recently rained, you might be able to see erosion in action as water finds its way across fields, parking lots, and the playground, making little gullies in the ground. Has the water moved sediment?

CASE STUDY:
Adopt-A-Spot

The trick to understanding erosion is to study an area carefully and make regular observations. Erosion can be a big problem in some areas. Sometimes soil and sediment are carried away by water and leave gullies or uneven surfaces. Even landslides can occur.

1. Choose it.

Pick an area outside that is safe to regularly observe. Try to mark off about a 60 cm by 60 cm space.

2. Draw it.

Draw a detailed sketch of the area and record observations about soil, rocks, and any water that you might see. It might also be helpful to take a photo of your spot.

- *Do you notice any evidence of animals such as footprints?*
- *Are there any cracks in the ground? If so, measure and record their size.*

3. Revisit it.

Come back to your spot after one week and record your observations. Draw another sketch, or take another picture. Have you noticed any changes? Continue to come back every two weeks.

What have you noticed over time? Are there plantings such as grass or bushes that are helping to prevent erosion in your spot? Is erosion a problem? If erosion is a problem, what could you do to prevent further erosion or repair the area?

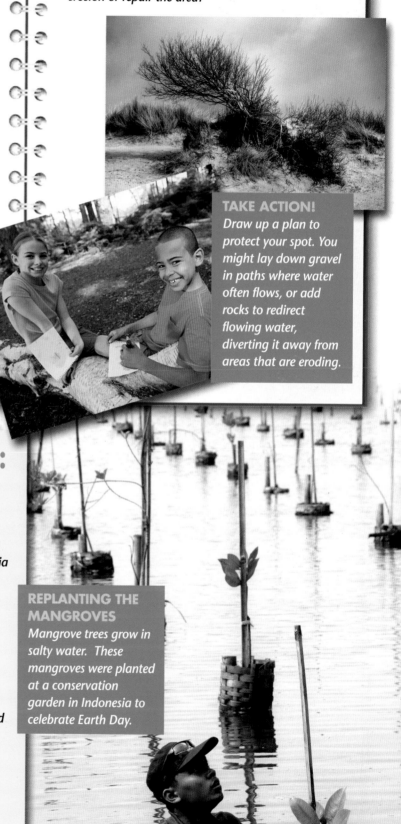

TAKE ACTION!
Draw up a plan to protect your spot. You might lay down gravel in paths where water often flows, or add rocks to redirect flowing water, diverting it away from areas that are eroding.

REPLANTING THE MANGROVES
Mangrove trees grow in salty water. These mangroves were planted at a conservation garden in Indonesia to celebrate Earth Day.

SCIENTIST IN THE SPOTLIGHT: A "FRIEND OF NATURE"

When Adeline Tiffanie Suwana was 11 years old, her village in Indonesia was hit by a devastating flood. She learned that the mangrove forests in her homeland, which had been chopped down for lumber, would have helped protect her village from this natural disaster. Soon after, Adeline organized a group of friends and started "Friends of Nature." Since then, her work has involved over 15,000 Indonesian students.

Adeline encouraged students to protect the coral reefs and to plant mangrove trees. She organized environmental cleanup and education days. Her focus is on reforestation, coral reef conservation, and developing sustainable energy.

Her determination has led to her to be a delegate to the United Nations Environment Programme as well as the subject of a TV documentary in her homeland. You are never too young to make a difference!

RECAP AND REVIEW

THREE DIFFERENT KINDS OF ROCK

Sedimentary Rock
Wind, water, or natural chemicals break the rock down into small pieces called sediments. These sediments move, get piled up, and cemented into layers.

Igneous Rock
Earth's intense heat melts the rock into a thick liquid which then cools back into a solid.

Metamorphic Rock
Rock that has been exposed to Earth's great heat and pressure deep in the crust causes the minerals that make up the rock to change shape.

THE ROCK CYCLE
Rock is always changing from one type to another.

Rock is weathered, eroded, and deposited to form sediment.

ROCKS TO KNOW

| Coal | Sandstone | Limestone | Shale | Granite | Obsidian | Gneiss | Slate |

EARTH'S FOUR LAYERS

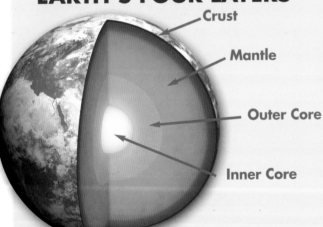

Crust

Mantle

Outer Core

Inner Core

FOSSILS
Fossils show evidence of a changing Earth.

A 500 million-year-old stromatolite— a kind of giant algae—found near Roanoke, Virginia.

WEATHERING
The breaking down of rock into smaller pieces by thawing and freezing, acids in nature, blowing grit, and burrowing animals.

EROSION AND DEPOSITION
The moving of rock fragments by wind and water, and the settling of those bits in a new location.

THREE TYPES OF TECTONIC PLATE BOUNDARIES

Divergent
Plates move apart.

Convergent
Plates move toward each other.

Transform
Plates slide alongside each other.

Use pages 136-137 to answer question 1.

1. Explain the quote, "Every rock on Earth is constantly moving and changing over time."

Use pages 138-139 to answer question 2.

2. How do scientists determine a rock type?

Use pages 140-141 to answer question 3.

3. Compare and contrast how sedimentary, igneous, and metamorphic rocks are created.

Use pages 142-143 to answer question 4.

4. Draw and label the rock cycle. Describe the major processes and rock types involved at each point of the rock cycle.

Use page 144-145 to answer question 5.

5. Copy and complete the chart. ⟶

Use pages 146-147 to answer question 6.

6. What information does fossil evidence provide to scientists?

Rock Type	What are some examples?	What does it look like?
Sedimentary		
Igneous		
Metamorphic		

Use pages 148-149 to answer questions 7 and 8.

7. Draw and label a diagram of Earth's layers.
8. How does Earth's interior affect its surface?

Use pages 150-151 to answer questions 9 and 10.

9. What are tectonic plates?
10. Why do certain parts of the world experience earthquakes and volcanic eruptions while other parts remain largely unaffected by these natural occurrences?

Use pages 152-153 to answer questions 11 and 12.

11. Name and describe the three types of plate tectonic boundaries.
12. How do plate tectonic boundaries affect the surface of the Earth? How do they affect the ocean floor?

Use pages 154-155 to answer question 13.

13. What causes an earthquake? How does an earthquake affect the Earth's surface?

Use pages 156-157 to answer question 14.

14. How does a volcano form? What impact does a volcanic eruption have on the Earth's surface?

Use pages 158-159 to answer question 15.

15. Explain the term weathering in relation to rock formation. How does weathering occur?

Use pages 160-161 to answer question 16.

16. What is the difference between erosion and deposition?

Use pages 162-163 to answer questions 17 and 18.

17. State an example of how people have changed the Earth's surface.
18. How can negative changes to the Earth's surface be controlled?

YOU ARE THE SCIENTIST

A seismologist is a scientist who studies earthquakes. Using the map on page 151, where would you suggest a seismologist might experience the most earthquake activity? Support your answer.

DATA DETETCTIVE

Study this chart showing earthquake activity in the U.S. between 2000-2010. What magnitude earthquakes occurred most frequently? What year saw the most earthquakes? What can you infer from the total number of earthquakes over the 10-year period?

Magnitude	2000	2001	2002	2003	2004	2005	2006	2007	2008	2009	2010
8.0-9.9	0	0	0	0	0	0	0	0	0	0	0
7.0-7.9	0	1	1	2	0	1	0	1	0	0	1
6.0-6.9	6	5	4	7	2	4	7	9	9	4	8
5.0-5.9	63	41	63	54	25	47	51	72	85	58	81
4.0-4.9	917	842	1535	1303	1362	1475	1213	1137	1486	1492	3586
3.0-3.9	917	842	1535	1303	1362	1475	1213	1137	1486	1492	3586
2.0-2.9	660	646	1228	704	1336	1738	1145	1173	1573	2379	4130
1.0-1.9	0	2	2	2	1	2	7	11	13	26	39
0.1-0.9	0	0	0	0	0	0	1	0	0	1	0
Total	2342	2261	3876	2946	3550	3685	2783	2791	3618	4262	8497

There are many more 0.1-1.9 earthquakes but smaller earthquakes are very hard to detect and record.

CHAPTER EIGHT

RESOURCES

Additional information
to help you use
Exploring Science:
All Around Us

GLOSSARY

Abyssal plain: A very wide, very flat section of the deep ocean floor made of thick layers of sediment.

Adaptations: Physical characteristics and behaviors that allow plants and animals to satisfy life's needs and respond to the environment.

Atom: The smallest unit of an element.

Balance: A measurement tool with balanced beam and two pans used to weigh an object and determine its mass.

Camouflage: A structural adaptation that lets an animal blend into an environment so that it is almost impossible to see.

Cell: The smallest unit of life. Some organisms are made of just one cell. Others are made of many cells.

Cell membrane: The outside layer of a cell that controls what goes in and out of the cell.

Cell wall: An outer layer of a plant cell that provides extra support.

Chloroplast: A cell part in plants that makes food for the cell.

Classification key: The classification and naming of animals, plants, minerals, and rocks in an ordered system that shows their natural relationships.

Compound: A substance made of at least two different elements bonded together.

Compression wave: Another terms for a longitudinal sound wave in which the air gets bunched up or compressed.

Constants: Things that remain the same on purpose during an experiment.

Continental rise: The area of the ocean at the bottom of the continental slope. It is a vast underwater hill made from tons of accumulated sediment.

Continental shelf: The underwater edge of a continent.

Continental slope: A steep slope that separates the continental shelf from the deep ocean basin.

Control: The part of an experiment where the independent variable is left unchanged to provide a comparison.

Convergent boundary: A place where the Earth's tectonic plates push against each other.

Core: The center of the Earth. It's outer and an inner cores are composed mostly of iron and nickel. The outer core is fluid; the inner core is solid.

Crest: The peak or top of a light or water wave.

Crust: The upper layer of the Earth on which we live. The crust is broken into pieces called tectonic plates that float on the next layer—the mantle.

Current: A body of water moving very quickly in a definite direction through surrounding waters that are moving more slowly. Currents are caused by wind patterns and differences in water densities.

Cytoplasm: The fluid inside a cell.

Data: All the facts, descriptions, and numbers collected during an experiment.

Decibel: A unit used to measure the loudness of sounds on a scale from zero to 150. Sounds at the higher decibel ranges can permanently damage your ears.

Density: The measure of how much mass is contained in a solid object, liquid, or gas and how tightly the molecules are packed. With some materials, such as liquids and gases, the density can be changed. With solid objects, the density cannot be changed.

Dependent variable: Something in an experiment that can be measured or observed to see how it responds to a change made to the independent variable.

Deposition: The process by which sediment, which has been transported by natural forces like wind, water, ice, and gravity, is dropped or finally deposited somewhere on the Earth's surface.

Depth: A deep place in a body of water.

Divergent boundary: A place where the Earth's tectonic plates are moving away from each other.

Dormancy: A period of inactivity.

Earthquakes: The violent shaking of the Earth that occurs when a tectonic plate snaps.

Echolocation: The location of objects using reflected sound. Animals such as toothed whales, dolphins, and bats use echolocation.

Electromagnetic spectrum: The entire range of light energy. From longest to shortest, these wavelengths of light are: radio waves, microwaves, infrared waves, visible light waves, ultraviolet rays, X-rays, and gamma rays.

Electrons: Parts of an atom with a negative charge that swirl around the outside of the nucleus.

Element: Matter made of only one type of atom.

Epicenter: The location on the surface of the Earth directly above where an earthquake starts.

Erosion: The movement of rocks and soil from one place to another by the forces of gravity, water, ice, or wind.

Estimation: A rough or approximate calculation of the amount, size, or value of something.

Fault: A break in the Earth's crust that results in the ground moving along the line of the break.

Food web: All the interactions in which organisms eat each other in a community. Each sequence of what eats what is known as a food chain, and almost every chain starts with plants that are eaten by herbivores or omnivores.

Fossil: The preserved remains of an animal, plant, or other organism from some past geologic or prehistoric time.

Frequency: The number of wavelengths in a given amount of time.

Gas: Matter that has no definite volume, can be compressed, and flows easily. Its molecules are far apart and will expand to fill a container.

Geologist: A scientist who studies the Earth's physical structure and all the events that helped shape it.

Graduated cylinder: A narrow, round container used to precisely measure the volume of a liquid.

Gravity: A pulling force between objects. The more massive the object, the stronger the pull.

Gulf Stream: A powerful, warm, and swift ocean current flowing from the Gulf of Mexico at the tip of Florida along the coastline of the United States and then eastward across the North Atlantic.

Hertz: The system for measuring frequency of sound and radio waves. One hertz is equal to one vibration per second.

Hibernation: A deep winter sleep that allows an animal's body to slow down so much that it can survive without eating or drinking.

Hypothesis: An explanation based on scientific reasoning that can be tested to see if it is correct. A hypothesis usually starts with an "If."

Igneous rock: Rocks that form when hot magma or lava cool and harden.

Independent variable: Something changed in an experiment on purpose to see how it affects the outcome.

Inference: A conclusion based on evidence about what has already occurred.

Infrared: Wavelengths slightly longer than those of visible red light and shorter than those of microwaves and radio waves.

Infrasound: Sound that has a frequency below the range of human hearing.

Invertebrate: An animal without a backbone.

Lava: Magma that has erupted from a volcano or a fissure in the Earth's crust.

Light: A form of energy that our eyes can detect.

Liquid: A fluid form of matter that takes the shape of a container, has a definite volume, is not easy to compress, and flows easily.

Longitudinal wave: Another term for a compression wave in which the air gets bunched up or compressed.

Magma: Molten rock below or within the Earth's crust. When magma erupts onto the Earth's surface, it is called lava.

Mantle: The thickest layer of the Earth, directly under the crust. It is composed of very hot, dense rock on which the tectonic plates float.

Mass: A measure of the amount of matter in an object.

Matter: Anything that has mass and takes up space.

Metamorphic rock: Created when rock deep in the Earth's crust is exposed to so much heat and pressure that it changes into something new.

Metric System: A way of measuring dimensions, distance, mass, and volume used by scientists around the world and based on the number 10.

Microscope: A device used to magnify and examine the details of small objects, even things too small to be seen by the human eye.

Mimicry: A structural adaptation that lets certain species look like other more dangerous ones.

Minerals: Solid, pure substances that can be found in the Earth's crust. Every rock on Earth is made of a combination of different minerals.

Mitochondria: Tiny power centers of plant and animal cells that convert sugars into usable energy for the cell.

Mixture: A combination of two or more pure substances that are not bonded together and can be separated by physical methods.

Model: A three-dimensional representation of something.

Molecule: A combination of atoms bonded together. A molecule is the smallest part of a substance that is made up of two or more atoms. The smallest unit of a compound.

Multicellular organism: Made of more than one cell.

Neutrons: Parts of an atom that have no charge and are part of the nucleus.

Nonvascular plant: A plant without a system to transport water and food to its cells.

Nucleus: In an organism, the control center in both animal and plant cells. In an atom, the central portion made of protons and neutrons.

Observation: The basis for forming a hypothesis based on something you see, feel, hear, taste, smell, or touch.

Ocean: Any of the five large bodies of salt water that cover the Earth's surface. The depth, salinity, and the temperature of the ocean affect where the different types of marine organisms can live.

Opaque: Stopping light from passing through.

Organism: Any living thing such as a plant, animal, fungus, yeast, or bacterium.

Phytoplankton: Tiny plant-like organisms that form the base of the ocean food web.

Pitch: How high or how low a sound is. This is determined by the frequency.

Plankton: Tiny, free floating organisms that are the basis of the ocean food web. There are two types: plant-like phytoplankton and animal-like zooplankton.

Prediction: An educated guess about what you expect to happen in the future based on past experience and careful observation.

Prism: An object that refracts and disperses white light into visible light.

Protons: Parts of an atom with a positive charge that are part of the nucleus.

Qualitative data: Descriptions of what can be observed, such as relative size, color, shape, smell, or other properties. It does not rely on measuring tools.

Quantitative data: Descriptions using number measurements such as width, height, volume, speed, or temperature.

Rarefaction: The opposite of compression. Places where molecules of air are not squeezed and are spread out.

Reflection: The bouncing of light off an object. Also the return of sound waves from a surface as in echolocation.

Refraction: The bending of light as it passes from one medium to another.

Richter scale: Used to measure the amount of energy released by an earthquake.

Rock cycle: The continuous process by which new rock is made and old rock is destroyed or changed from one form to another. The three forms of rock are metamorphic, sedimentary, and igneous.

Salinity: A measure of the amount of salt in the ocean's waters.

Scientific method: A systematic approach to learning about the world by identifying a question or problem; developing a hypothesis and designing an experiment to test it; and then carefully observing, recording, and analyzing the results.

Sediment: The small particles of weathered rock carried away by wind and water. Sediment also can come from decomposed plants and animals that have drifted down to the bottom of a body of water.

Sedimentary rock: Formed by layers of rock that have been eroded and then pressed together and hardened.

Solid: Matter that keeps a fixed shape, has a definite volume, and is not easy to compress. Its molecules are packed closely together.

Solution: A mixture in which one substance dissolves in another.

Sound waves: Alternating areas of high and low pressure, also called compression waves. Each sound wave has three important parts that create a distinct sound: how wide the wave length, how often it repeats, and how tall it is. Sound waves only travel where there is matter to transmit them.

Sound: A form of energy made by vibrations that travel through the air or another medium and can be heard when they reach a person's or animal's ear.

Tectonic plates: Parts of the Earth's crust that rest on the very dense hot rock of the mantle. As they float around, the plates can pull apart at a divergent boundary, slide next to each other at a transform boundary, or move toward each other at a convergent boundary.

Tension: A pulling force exerted by one object on another object. Tension is one of the factors in creating pitch, along with the length and thickness of the object that is vibrating and the amount of air it moves.

Tides: The rising and falling water levels of oceans, bays, gulfs, and parts of many rivers caused by the forces of gravity between the Earth, the moon, and the sun.

Transform boundary: A place where the Earth's plates slide alongside each other.

Translucent: Allowing some light to pass through.

Transparent: Allowing light to pass through easily.

Transverse wave: A wave that moves up and down at the same time it moves forward. Light travels this way.

Trench: A very long and narrow canyon-like depression deep in the ocean floor.

Trend: The general direction in which data is headed or the way it is changing.

Trough: The bottom of a light or water wave.

Tsunami: A huge surge of water caused by earthquakes or volcanic eruptions under the sea. As the tsunami approaches a coastline, the large mass of water rushing onshore is so powerful it destroys everything in its path.

Ultrasound: Sound that has a frequency above the range of human hearing.

Unicellular organism: Made of only one cell.

Vacuole: The part of a cell that stores food, water, and waste.

Vacuum: A space with absolutely no matter. Sound cannot travel in a vacuum like that on the moon or elsewhere in outer space.

Variable: Something that can be changed in an experiment.

Vascular plant: A plant with a system to transport water and food to its cells.

Vertebrate: An animal with a backbone.

Vibration: A back and forth movement of an object.

Volcano: A vent in the Earth's crust through which magma, steam, and ash are violently expelled.

Volume: The amount of space a solid, liquid, or gas occupies.

Wavelength: In sound waves, the distance between two compressions or two rarefactions. In light waves, the distance between two crests or two troughs.

Waves: Created by wind blowing over a body of water's surface. The size of the waves depends on the speed of the wind and how far it can travel unobstructed.

Weathering: The wearing down and breaking up of hard rock by natural forces like wind, ice, plants, and burrowing animals.

Weight: A measure of the gravitational pull on an object.

Zooplankton: Tiny animal-like creatures that drift or move with ocean currents. They survive on other plankton, but also provide food for many ocean creatures including the largest—the blue whale.

CONVERSION CHART

Length

1 centimeter (cm) = 10 millimeters (mm)

1 meter (m) =100 centimeters (cm)

1 kilometer (km) = 1000 meters (m)

---

1 inch = 2.54 centimeters (cm)

1 foot = 0.30 meters (m)

1 meter (m) = 3.28 feet

1 kilometer (km) = 0.6 miles

1 mile = 1.6 kilometers (km)

Speed

1 mile per hour (mph) = 1.6 kilometers per hour

1 kilometer per hour = 0.62 miles per hour

Volume

1 liter (l) = 1000 milliliters (ml)

---

1 fluid ounce = 29.6 milliliters (ml)

1 liter (l) = 33.8 fluid ounces

1 gallon = 3.8 liters

Mass

1 milligram (mg) = 0.001 grams (g)

1 gram (g) = 0.001 kilograms (kg)

1 kilogram (kg) = 1000 grams

---

1 gram (g) = 0.035 ounces

1 ounce = 28.35 grams (g)

1 pound (lb) = 0.45 kilograms (kg)

1 kilogram (kg) = 2.2 pounds (lb)

1 ton = 2000 pounds

1 metric ton = 1000 kilograms (kg)

Temperature

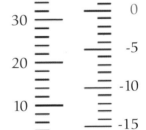

PARTS OF A MICROSCOPE

Microscopes can vary in design, but they all have the same basic parts. This diagram will help you familiarize yourself with the different pieces.

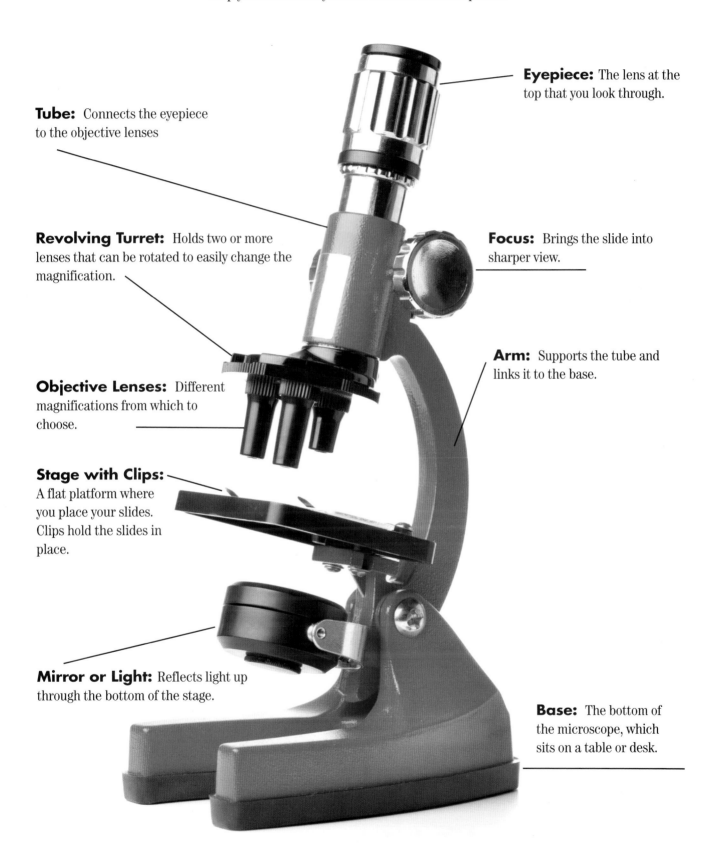

Tube: Connects the eyepiece to the objective lenses

Revolving Turret: Holds two or more lenses that can be rotated to easily change the magnification.

Objective Lenses: Different magnifications from which to choose.

Stage with Clips: A flat platform where you place your slides. Clips hold the slides in place.

Mirror or Light: Reflects light up through the bottom of the stage.

Eyepiece: The lens at the top that you look through.

Focus: Brings the slide into sharper view.

Arm: Supports the tube and links it to the base.

Base: The bottom of the microscope, which sits on a table or desk.

INDEX

PICTURE CREDITS

Despite extensive research it is not always possible to establish property ownership/copyright. When this is the case we would appreciate notification.

All photos and photo-illustrations are from Shutterstock Images with the exception of the following: Cover: top, Getty Images; Page 4: lower left, Blend Images; Page 5: Photoresearchers; Page 8: top right, Corbis; Page 9: middle left, Donna Coveney/MIT, top right, NASA, middle right, Sean Flynn/UConn Photo; Page 10: top left, Neal Snyder/U.S. Army Environmental Command, bottom right, Photoresearchers; Page 12: bottom right, MSA; Page 15: bottom left, Getty Images; Page 27: CymaScope.com/John Stuart Reid/BakerComarsh; Page 29: middle top, Photoresearchers; Page 30: bottom left, Getty Images, bottom right, MSA; Page 33: bottom, Photoresearchers; Page 35: top left, U.S. Navy photo by John Gay; Page 37: top left, Design Pics; Page 38: top, Corbis; Page 40: bottom, NASA; Page 42: middle right, Photoresearchers; Page 43: middle left, Getty Images; Page 49: bottom left, Rodrigo Beleia, bottom right, Minden Pictures; Page 50: bottom right, Wired Magazine; Page 53: top left, University of New South Wales, middle right, DK Images; Page 59: top right, Blend Images, middle left, NASA; Page 60: middle left, Photoresearchers; Page 71: bottom row, all Photoresearchers; Page 73: top, Photoresearchers; Page 78: top right, Photoresearchers; Page 82: middle right, Photoresearchers; Page 91: center, Photoresearchers; Page 92: all cell art is Photoresearchers; Page 94: middle, Bill Graham; bottom left, David S. Godsell, the Scripps Research Institute; Page 95: all Bill Graham, Page 96: middle right, Photoresearchers; Page 97, middle, Photoresearchers; bottom right, Virginia Tech/ College of Engineering; Page 102: middle, Photoresearchers; Page 104: middle right series. Mark Payne-Gil/Nature Picture Library, bottom left, Greendiary; Page 105: bottom left, Paul Prescott/Shutterstock; bottom right, Flip Nicklin/Minden Pictures; Page 111: middle right, Photoresearchers, bottom right, APF; Pages 112-113: all Don Dixon/ Cosmo-graphica; Pages 114-115: top map, Marie Tharp Maps, LLC, 114: bottom, Don Dixon; Page 115, bottom middle, NOAA; Page 116: top right, Marie Tharp Maps, LLC, bottom, Don Dixon; Page 117: middle left, Don Dixon, middle right, Photoresearchers, bottom, Don Dixon; Page 119: top, Photoresearchers, middle and bottom left, NOAA; Page 121: bottom right, TK; Page 123: top right, Mainichi Shimbun/Reuters; middle right, Thinkstock; Page 124: middle right, Michele Davino / Barcroft Media, bottom left,NIWA ; Page 125: top left, Don Dixon, bottom left, Marine Resources Research Institute/SERTC; middle right, Minden Images, bottom right, NIWA; Page 127: middle: Jeremy A. Goldbogen & Nicholas D. Pyenson, middle right, Photoresearchers; Page 128: Smithsonion Museum of Natural History; Page 129: top right, NASA, middle, Uppsala Biomedical Center; Page 131: bottom right, Photoresearchers; Page 136: top, C Productions, bottom, Naica Caves; Page 140: top right, Hulton-Deutsch Collection/Corbis; Page 146: middle right, Jeffrey Mankie/News & Messenger, bottom left, Berni Nonenmacher; Page 147: dinosaur fossil illustrations by Bill Graham, middle right, TK; Page 148: top, Photoresearchers; Page 149: bottom left, Karsten Pedersen/University of Gothenburg, Sweden, middle right, Peter Sforza; Page 150: bottom, Corbis; Page 151: NASA, bottom right map, USGS; Page 152: top, Corbis; Page 154: AP Photo/George Nikitin; Page 155: top right, Xinhua/Wang Fengfeng, bottom right, Yomiuri Shimbun, AFP/Getty Images; Page 156 bottom left, Photoresearchers; Page 157 top right, Photoresearchers, middle left, National Geographic Stock, bottom right, Granger; Page 163: bottom left, Action for Nature, bottom right, Corbis Back cover: bottom left, Chen Wei Seng/Shutterstock